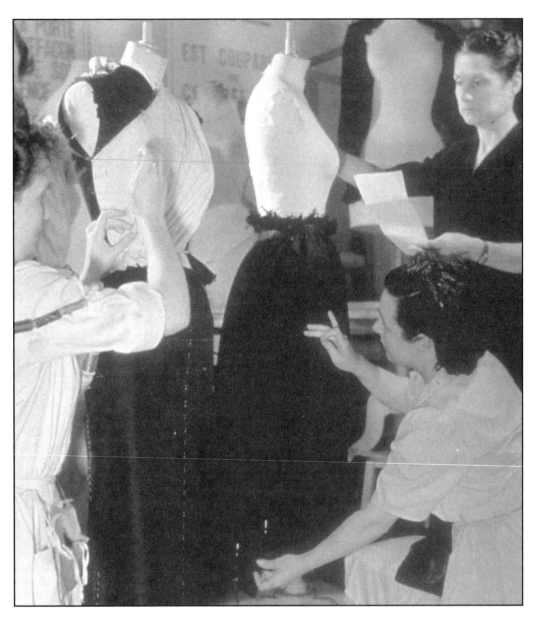

The fashion business includes not only the designers who dream up new clothes, but also the many people who make and sell the finished products. The revolutionary "New Look" introduced by Christian Dior in 1947 would not have been possible without the seamstresses shown here, who crafted dresses based on his sketches.

BUSINESS BUILDERS
IN FASHION

Jacqueline C. Kent

The Oliver Press, Inc.
Minneapolis

For Nica and Jonathan, dreams do come true.

The Oliver Press, Inc.
Charlotte Square
5707 West 36th Street
Minneapolis, MN 55416-2510

Library of Congress Cataloging-in-Publication Data
Kent, Jacqueline, 1960-
Business builders in fashion/Jacqueline Kent.
p. cm. — (Business builders ; 5)
Includes bibliographical references and index.
ISBN 1-881508-80-3
1. Fashion designers—Biography. 2. Fashion—History. I. Title. II. Series.
TT505.A1 K46 2003
746.9'2'0922—dc21
[B]   2001059313
                                                CIP
                                                        AC

ISBN 1-881508-80-3
Printed in the United States of America

09 08 07 06 05 04 03   8 7 6 5 4 3 2 1

Contents

Introduction

HAUTE COUTURE TO READY-TO-WEAR

A tall, thin model struts down the runway and turns to each side, showing off the latest designer clothes. Writers, photographers, and buyers for department stores look on intently, scribbling or clicking away as they try to record the details of every outfit. Runway shows such as this are an important part of today's fashion business, but they are nowhere near the only part. The fashion world includes not only high-profile designers and supermodels, but also the textile industry, clothing and accessory manufacturers, advertising agencies, fashion magazines, retail and wholesale groups, and numerous other professions.

This booming industry has developed in part out of simple necessity. Human beings have always needed to protect themselves from heat, cold, rain,

textile: a fabric, especially one made by weaving or knitting

As journalists and photographers crowd near, models display outfits by designer Gianni Versace at a 1990 runway show in Milan, Italy—one of the world's fashion centers.

and snow. But fashion also serves other purposes. For centuries, fashion has been an important way for men and women to express themselves. People who have a simple approach to life tend to wear simple clothes, while those who love pomp and show choose clothes that shout to the world. Fashion can provide comfort, but it also offers opportunities for glittering, glamorous display.

HAUTE COUTURE AND READY-TO-WEAR

Today's fashion industry can be divided into two main areas: haute couture and ready-to-wear. Haute couture (pronounced OTE koo-TUR), French for "high or elegant sewing," is fashion that is made to order—constructed to fit one individual perfectly. When a couture designer, such as Vera Wang, creates a garment for a client, such as the bridal gown Wang designed for actor Sharon Stone, the design involves intricate hand-stitching, which is difficult to mass-produce. Couture designers, or couturiers, often use the most luxurious, expensive fabrics, and they always pay careful attention to how the fabric is cut. Haute couture designs are sewn by very skilled people and are extremely expensive to create. Some couturiers even consider haute couture to be more of an art than a business, with their creations meant to be gazed at and admired, rather than actually worn.

Ready-to-wear fashion, on the other hand, takes many different forms. Sometimes it is mass-produced for sale to stores around the world, and other times it is made in smaller quantities for very special stores. In any case, ready-to-wear is always made in standard sizes so that a customer can go into a store, try on an outfit, and take it home immediately.

Fashion designers can be loosely grouped into the same two categories: those who design haute couture, like Jean-Paul Gaultier in France, and those who design ready-to-wear, like Calvin Klein in the United States. Still, most haute couture designers eventually venture into the world of ready-to-wear, because the market is simply too lucrative to ignore.

Many of the most fantastic creations of haute couture are not meant for comfort or for practical use. This minidress, for example— designed by Paco Rabanne in 1968—is made of aluminum.

EARLY CLOTHING

Long before ready-to-wear fashion or haute couture existed, our ancestors had to find ways to stay warm when it snowed, dry when it rained, and cool when the sun blazed down on their bare skin. The earliest kinds of clothing were probably made from the skins of animals. People draped them around their bodies just as we drape a shawl or an afghan today. The early Eskimos learned how to sew seams together using a piece of bone or ivory as a needle. The Eskimos were thus able to make the first fitted garments, clothes sewn to their body measurements.

Once civilizations had figured out the best way to protect their bodies from the weather, they realized there were other things they could do with clothes. They experimented with colors and styles and added shells, flowers, and pretty stones. In ancient Egypt, where it was very hot during the day, people liked lightweight cotton and linen garments. They sometimes wore only short skirts or loincloths. In ancient Rome, men wore togas, long pieces of fabric that they draped around their bodies in elaborate folds. Styles of draping, colors, and size all gave indications of the wearer's age and status.

loincloth: a strip of fabric worn over the loins, or pelvic area

OBTAINING CLOTHING

Up until very recently in history, individual families were responsible for supplying their own clothes. In the Middle Ages in Europe, lower-class women generally made clothing for their families or had to gather castoff garments. The upper classes hired sewing women to make their undergarments, plus clothes for their children. These seamstresses also did the family's alterations. When a wealthy woman needed a new gown, however, she sent for a tailor. In addition to making beautiful dresses and coats for the lady of the house, the tailor supplied her husband with his entire wardrobe. At the time, only men were allowed to work as tailors.

Just after 1675, a law was passed in France that allowed women to become dressmakers. Women could complete a three-year apprenticeship with an experienced tailor to learn the arts of cutting fabric

In this sixteenth-century tailor's shop, the tailor fits a dress for a woman while his assistants sew other clothing items.

and dressmaking. At the end of her apprenticeship, a woman was considered a professional and could make a family's most important clothes. More and more women took advantage of this opportunity, and the job of dressmaking for upper-class ladies slowly shifted from men to women.

SUMPTUARY LAWS

Silk and other fabrics from Asia had been available in Europe for centuries, but only to the wealthy who could afford to import them along the 4,000-mile overland trade route known as the Silk Road. These exotic, highly prized materials were used to make luxurious clothes embroidered with beautiful designs and sewn with precious jewels. Such garments were status symbols, distinguishing the rich from the poor.

Around the turn of the sixteenth century, however, European explorers began to discover sea routes to Asia, making imported fabrics more widely available. Laws to restrict dress, called sumptuary laws, were created to make sure lower-class people did not start wearing fancy clothing. The Act for Reformation of Excess in Apparel was instituted in England in 1532. The Act assigned styles of dress to people by their level of income, forcing poor people to wear clothes that reflected their poverty. But it was a hard law to enforce, and people were always breaking it by dressing "above their class."

Sumptuary laws also existed in the early years of the American colonies. In the 1630s, Massachusetts law restricted the amount of trimmings and accessories a person could display, especially items such as gold, silver, and lace. Religious leaders also spoke out against lavish clothes, which many considered a sign of vanity. But once the colonies became the United States, the newly independent country instituted a government based on liberty and the pursuit of happiness, and people were free to wear what they wanted. The Americans eagerly awaited news of the latest European fashions.

FRANCE: THE CENTER OF FASHION

Beginning in the 1500s, European fashion was based on that of the royal court in France. The queen and her ladies decided what they wanted to wear, and court dressmakers produced the garments based on their descriptions. Once a new style was worn by the aristocracy, women all the way down the social ladder copied the design. The style then spread to different countries across Europe before finally landing in America.

In the 1860s, however, Charles Frederick Worth shifted the creation of fashion from the French aristocracy to couture designers. Instead of making a dress as it was described to him, Worth created his own designs and presented them to Parisian ladies. The couture house, where dresses were made to order and fitted to one particular woman, emerged.

INDUSTRIAL REVOLUTION AND READY-TO-WEAR

In the nineteenth century, an important development began to affect the fashion industry: the Industrial Revolution. Beginning in the 1700s in England, people had invented machines that would

Clothing designs created in France initially traveled through Europe and across the ocean to America in the form of "fashion babies." These small dolls were elegantly dressed in the latest Paris fashions, even down to the jewels that completed the outfit. Seamstresses could study the dolls and copy the dresses they wore for their customers. Eventually, designers began selling patterns of their clothing instead, giving seamstresses a more efficient way to produce their own versions of Paris fashions.

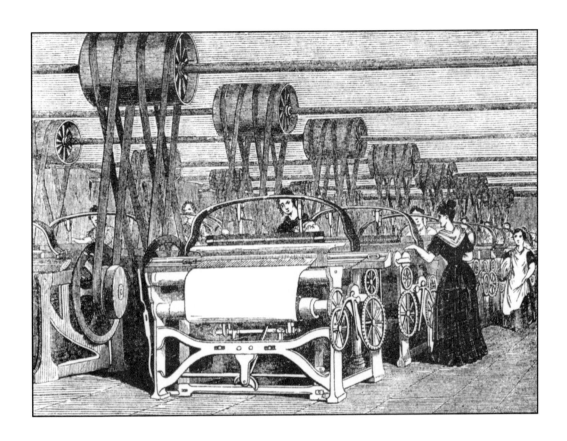

One of the major advances of the Industrial Revolution was the power loom, invented around 1785 to weave cloth automatically.

do many jobs more easily and faster than human labor could, including spinning yarn and weaving textiles. As a result, fabric became available in larger quantities and was less expensive. Factory jobs for lower-class women increased, which gave the women more money to spend. Many businessmen became newly wealthy from the innovations. Both groups wanted to spend their money on clothing. The women working in the factories didn't have time to sew their own clothes, and the businessmen wanted to make sure their wives were well dressed. The demand for ready-made clothing increased.

Some hand-sewn, ready-made dresses had been available in the United States as early as the 1820s, but machines had the potential to make garments much more quickly and in greater quantities. Between 1832 and 1877, many people worked on inventing or improving the sewing machine. Elias Howe patented the first modern sewing machine in 1846, and Isaac Singer perfected and promoted the machine for home use in the 1850s. Working on their home sewing machines, women could create more clothes than they needed for their own families and then offer the extra clothes for sale. The ready-made market began to grow.

Isaac Merritt Singer (1811-1875) created his first sewing machine in 1850. It featured an overhanging arm to hold the needle as it moved up and down, a table to support the cloth, a vertical bar to hold the cloth down, and a treadle (foot pedal) to generate power. Though innovative, the design borrowed heavily from Elias Howe—who successfully sued Singer and others for patent infringement in 1854. Despite this, the Singer Sewing Machine Company went on to become one of the world's largest manufacturers of personal sewing machines.

Home Sewing Patterns

Making clothing became even easier with the invention of the graded sewing pattern by an American tailor named Ebenezer Butterick. Patterns that people could use as guides for sewing clothes had existed before, but they only came in one size; people had to grade (enlarge or reduce) a pattern to the size of the wearer. Most people simply took apart their old, worn-out clothes and used them as models for new ones. In 1863, when Ellen Butterick suggested to her husband that making clothes for their infant son would be much easier if the patterns were his size, Ebenezer began experimenting. He developed graded patterns made of tissue paper, which the Buttericks cut, folded, and sold from their home. Business was booming within a year, and other pattern companies soon sprang up to take advantage of the growing market.

Graded patterns helped make fashion more widely available. People who could not afford haute couture or who lived far from the nearest store could still create clothes in the latest styles with the aid of mass-produced patterns. Even after ready-made clothing became the norm for most people, home sewing patterns continued to sell, especially in times of economic difficulty such as the Great Depression and World War II.

In 1949, home sewing met haute couture when Vogue Patterns—an offshoot of the popular fashion magazine—became the first company to base patterns on collections by Paris couturiers. Since then, Vogue Patterns (now owned by E. Butterick & Co.) has been licensed to produce sewing patterns designed by leading fashion figures such as Yves Saint Laurent, Hubert de Givenchy, Oscar de la Renta, Calvin Klein, Donna Karan, and Bill Blass. Selling their designs as patterns that people can reproduce at home allows these couturiers to reach a wider variety of customers with their creations.

In the late 1880s, women's suits—consisting of a long skirt, a jacket, and a blouse—became fashionable. Eventually, women discarded the jackets and simply wore the blouses, known as shirtwaists, tucked into their skirts. Thus began the first fashion craze. Newly opened factories quickly produced shirtwaists in all sizes and sold them to working

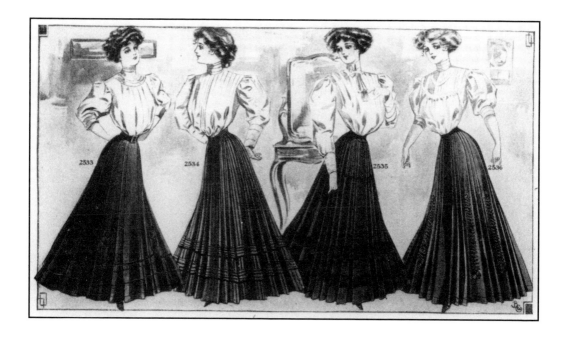

women. From blouses, the new industry eventually moved to manufacturing dresses, and soon, almost every garment imaginable was mass-produced.

SEVENTH AVENUE AND NATIONAL PRESS WEEK

As more and more clothing was made in factories, New York City developed into the center of the American garment industry. Since the 1920s, New York's Seventh Avenue—an entire district between 36th and 42nd Streets—has housed almost all the American ready-to-wear manufacturers. The companies are grouped in specific areas based on the kind of clothes they make and how much their products cost. This way, buyers can focus on a specific price range when selecting merchandise for their stores.

With their shirtwaists, tightly cinched waists, toe-length skirts, and upswept hair, these clothing-catalog models typify the "Gibson girl" fashion of the late nineteenth and early twentieth centuries. The style was named after illustrator Charles Dana Gibson, who drew beautiful, idealized women for popular magazines such as Harper's.

Men pull racks of clothing along a sidewalk in New York's Seventh Avenue area—often known as the Garment District—in 1955.

American fashion designers also generally work from New York. During National Press Week, a Seventh Avenue tradition since 1941, designers show their newest designs for spring and fall in electrifying, dramatic, and highly staged fashion shows. In addition to displaying one-of-a-kind items, designers show clothes that can be made and sold in large quantities. All of these clothes sell for very high prices. Fashion editors, photographers, and buyers all gather at the Seventh Avenue shows to see the latest clothing lines. Then the buyers choose the designs they think will sell in their stores.

LOW-END READY-TO-WEAR

At the other end of the ready-to-wear spectrum, a number of companies manufacture inexpensive clothing—often copies of designer originals—to sell to low-end department stores. Manufacturers use sophisticated merchandising plans and computer-based analysis to predict what will sell each season. Then, based on the results of the analysis, they quickly produce merchandise and deliver it by truck to local stores, where it is tagged, steamed to get rid of wrinkles, and placed on racks or shelves, ready for the customer to buy. All this must be done before the consumers' tastes change and before new trends in style or color replace the current ones.

INFLUENTIAL DESIGNERS

The fashion designers profiled in the following chapters have contributed to the rise of the business of fashion and its development into the mammoth industry we know today. Some of the designers discussed include Charles Worth, who introduced high fashion in the nineteenth century; Gabrielle Chanel, whose relaxed yet stylish clothing reflected women's growing personal freedoms in the 1920s; and Levi Strauss, who built a worldwide business with his comfortable, useful denim pants. Through these stories, it is possible to see not only how fashion designers can become personally successful, but also how they can influence both the fashion industry and the societies in which they live.

1

CHARLES FREDERICK WORTH

THE FATHER OF
HAUTE COUTURE

"To the right, madame."

The woman stepped to her right and pivoted until she faced the small man. The only sound in the room was the swishing of her skirts as they settled into place after her turn.

"To the left. In front."

She did as she was told, trying not to become irritated. As the wife of one of the wealthiest men in France, she could afford to have any dressmaker brought to her home at a moment's notice to make her gowns. But she knew that no matter how beautiful the dress might be, it would not be noticed at all if it had not been made by Charles Worth.

Charles Frederick Worth (1825-1895), who set the trends for upper-class women in the latter half of the nineteenth century, is known as the first true fashion designer.

She remembered the days before Worth's arrival in France, when fashion had been determined by the ladies of the royal court. But once Worth had established himself as a designer, he had created dresses of his own choosing, rather than simply making what the queen or her ladies selected. Now everything was different. Not only did Worth decide what he would design, but he also decided who he would design for. She had needed a referral from a friend to see him. With his elegant dresses, Worth had created haute couture, or high fashion—clothes tailored to fit their wearers perfectly. As if this were not remarkable enough, Charles Worth was not French, as might be expected (since all the fashionable designs came out of France), but English.

AN ENGLISHMAN IN PARIS

Charles Frederick Worth was born on October 13, 1825, in Bourne, a small English town in South Lincolnshire. His grandfather, father, and brother were all lawyers, and he might have followed them in their choice of profession if he had had the chance. But when Charles was about 11 years old, his father, who had always been a gambling man, lost all of the family's money. His mother, forced to work as a housekeeper, struggled to put food on the table.

Charles's future did not look promising. His mother sent him to work as an apprentice in a printer's shop, hoping that he would be able to make a decent living when he completed his training. The work was filthy, and Charles hated it. He begged his mother to find him something else. When Charles turned 13, his mother apprenticed him to a draper in London, where he learned how to sell fabric. The firm, Swan and Edgar, was located in Piccadilly Circus, a fashionable section of London where all of the best fabric shops and dressmakers' salons were located. Men as well as women purchased expensive fabrics at the drapers' stores and then took them next door to their tailors and dressmakers to have them made into the latest styles of clothing. Charles Worth served his seven-year apprenticeship selling

draper: a dealer in cloth

A London draper's shop assistant shows a customer some fabric in this 1841 drawing.

fabrics to these wealthy people. As a result, he became an expert at understanding which fabrics worked best for making what garments.

When he completed his apprenticeship in 1845, Worth went to work for Lewis and Allenby, the finest silk merchant in London. Lewis and Allenby supplied Queen Victoria with exquisite fabrics for her gowns. Despite Lewis and Allenby's reputation in England, Worth knew that if he wanted to be at the center of the fashion world, he would have to move to France. At the age of 20, he borrowed some money and left for Paris. Worth spent his first two years there studying French in the hope of eventually being hired by a fine French establishment.

A POSITION AT GAGELIN

Worth's hard work paid off when he was hired by Gagelin, one of the most famous mercers (dealers in textiles) in Paris. At Gagelin, Worth sold fine fabrics to wealthy ladies, just as he had done in London. His experience made him an expert at helping his customers select their fabrics.

At Gagelin, as in most fine textile establishments at the time, shawls and mantles were the only ready-made items sold. Shortly after he began working for them, Worth's employers moved him from selling fabrics to selling shawls, and Worth developed a particular trick he liked to play. After the whole shawl collection had been shown, he would comment that he had another, very exquisite shawl, but that he didn't think the customer would want to spend so much money. The customer would then want to see it right away. Worth would show one of the first shawls he had shown, now with an air of awe and reverence. The customer was more often than not inclined to buy the shawl.

Beautiful young women called "demoiselles de magasin" modeled the shawls. Worth fell in love with one of the models, Marie Vernet. To show how much he loved Marie, Worth created simple white muslin dresses for her. The beautiful shawls she modeled would thus be shown to their best possible advantage. Unexpectedly, the customers liked the simple dresses Marie wore, and they wanted Worth to create similar dresses for them. He knew he couldn't do it while selling shawls, so he asked his employers to allow him to start a dressmaking department in the store. After some resistance (dressmaking was considered beneath Gagelin), they relented, and, in 1850, Worth became a dressmaker.

DRESSMAKER

Worth's dresses were an immediate success, and his reputation for fabulous creations spread quickly among the ladies of Paris. For him, the quality of the fabric was the key to a beautifully made garment. Because his dressmaking department was part of a merchant's establishment rather than an independent dressmaking shop, Worth met directly with salesmen from textile mills, where fabrics were woven. This allowed him to request specific textiles for the dresses he wanted to make. Worth then designed his dresses to make the best use of the fabric he had selected. He used his knowledge of

Demoiselles de magasin were young girls around the age of 16 who had been apprenticed to a store by their parents. Their parents paid for their training and living expenses, and when their training was complete, the girls continued to work for the storeowner, eventually receiving a small salary. They often worked 12-hour days and had almost no life outside the shop.

Instead of showing his dresses in only one fabric as other designers did, Worth constructed the same dress in several fabrics to show how one design could be used for many different occasions.

English tailoring techniques, such as fitting the bodice (the upper part of a woman's dress) to her body and paying attention to the direction of the fabric's weave when cutting.

Worth also simplified and changed old tailoring techniques to find the best way to make a dress fit. As a result, his dresses fit their owners perfectly. Before Worth began designing clothing, even the wealthiest women's dresses had not fit them very well. Not only were Worth's customers pleased with their dresses, but his designs also won awards for his employers at two world exhibitions, at which countries gathered their best products for display.

Worth's decision to become a dressmaker was timed perfectly. Paris had recently become the capital of France's Second Empire, ruled by the pageantry-loving Napoleon III, who had seized power in 1851. He had immediately set about establishing a royal court and ordering public works, such as telegraph lines and new roads. This frenzy of activity ushered in a period of optimism, and French high society threw itself into a constant whirl of entertainment: state balls, imperial receptions, military parades, the opera. Ladies with busy social schedules needed many fine dresses, and Charles Worth was just the man to provide them.

WORTH AND BOBERGH

In spite of his success as a designer, Worth's employers never thought of him as more than a salesman. This became clear to him when he asked for a place on the store's board of directors and was turned

Worth became so well known for his superb workmanship that one customer noted, "What doesn't show is as good as what does, so that when the right side is quite worn out I shall simply wear the wrong side."

down. In 1851, Worth married Marie, and by 1856, they had two sons, Gaston and Jean Philippe. During both her pregnancies, in spite of Worth's objections, Gagelin's management forced Marie to work right up until she gave birth. With his new family responsibilities and his unhappiness at how he and Marie were being treated at Gagelin, Worth began to think about starting his own design business. He found another disgruntled salesman, Otto Gustave Bobergh, and together they opened Worth and Bobergh in 1858.

Marie Worth in about 1860

With his own establishment and an atmosphere of celebration in Paris, Worth needed only one more thing to secure his place as Paris's leading designer: a benefactor. Despite the reputation he had already begun to build as a dressmaker, he needed to find a highly ranked lady at court who would wear his dresses. If the other ladies liked her dresses, they would hire Worth to design theirs.

When the new Austrian ambassador to France arrived in Paris, Worth knew he was in luck. As soon as the ambassador's young wife, Princess Pauline von Metternich, arrived in 1859, Worth sent Marie to visit her with a book of his prettiest designs.

Worth could not visit Pauline von Metternich himself because Victorian society considered it improper for a man to talk to a woman about something so personal as her wardrobe. Worth, however, would soon change that.

Pauline von Metternich (1836-1921) with her husband, Prince Richard von Metternich (1829-1895), in about 1860

Princess Metternich was impressed with Worth's designs and ordered two gowns, one for daytime and one for evening, stipulating that neither dress should cost her more than 300 francs. Determined to please the princess, Worth created one of her gowns from a new and very expensive fabric called silk tulle, in white woven with silver. The gown cost much more to make than 300 francs, but Worth's decision to use the fabric paid off almost immediately. None other than the Empress Eugénie, wife of Napoleon III, noticed the dress when Princess Metternich wore it at the next royal ball. The empress asked Worth to meet with her the next day.

tulle: a fine, netlike, often starched fabric used to make veils, tutus, and gowns

DESIGNING FOR AN EMPRESS

At last, Worth had his chance to become an established designer. If the empress chose him as her personal designer, every other woman in Paris would want his dresses. He once again set to work to select a fabric that he could make into the perfect dress. Unfortunately, the brocade fabric he chose was one that the empress particularly disliked. She refused to accept the gown, and Worth would have lost his opportunity if Napoleon III had not entered the room during the fitting. The brocade was made in the city of Lyon, which had been hostile toward the emperor. Worth convinced Napoleon III that if the empress wore the dress, it would demonstrate Napoleon's desire to help the growth of the textile industry in Lyon. Such an honor to the city could win many supporters for the emperor. Napoleon ordered Eugénie to wear the dress.

brocade: a heavy fabric with a detailed, raised design

Spanish countess Eugénie de Montijo de Guzman (1826-1920) became empress when she married Napoleon III in 1853.

Despite this rocky beginning, Worth's other designs pleased the empress, and in 1860, she chose him as one of her personal designers. By 1864, Worth was her main designer, supplying all of her evening and state wear. Worth continued to persuade Eugénie to wear fabrics she normally would not have worn. Any fabric the empress wore became instantly popular with other French ladies. This was an enormous help to the textile manufacturers who made those particular fabrics. To show their gratitude to Worth, the textile manufacturers produced fabrics specifically for him.

Shortly after becoming the empress's primary designer, Worth found another way of introducing designs to the ladies of Paris. He dressed his wife and Princess Metternich in new styles and then sent them to Longchamps, a racecourse at which the best of society gathered. Here the new looks were admired, and, within days, other ladies were ordering their own versions.

Worth persuaded Marie to wear a bonnet without a flap at the back. The flap, called a bavolet, covered the back of the neck and had been popular for some time. Due to Worth's influence, the bavolet was entirely out of fashion by 1864.

This Worth ballgown from the 1860s is made of satin trimmed with tulle, swansdown, crystal beads, and glass pearls.

Worth's dresses, with their luxurious fabrics and intricate trimming, were beautiful to look at, but many of the changes he made were practical as well. Floor-length and cumbersome, nineteenth-century skirts dragged in the dirt when women took walks. In 1864, Worth raised hemlines on day dresses to the ankles. The empress loved the new style immediately. Worth also made crinolines go out of style. These large steel or whalebone cages had been worn underneath women's skirts to make them fuller.

A woman wearing a crinoline in about 1860. She is still in the process of dressing, waiting for the other women to help her put on her gown over the enormous hoops.

The Crinoline

In the 1840s, women liked the skirts of their dresses to be very full. To achieve this, they wore skirts underneath their dresses called petticoats. The number of heavy petticoats women wore slowly increased as wider and wider dresses became fashionable.

In 1856, when the weight of petticoats grew almost too much to bear, a new under-garment was introduced: the crinoline. This series of steel or whalebone hoops, linked together to form a kind of cage, caused the skirt of a dress to bulge outward—making it seem that there were still many petticoats underneath. The crinoline was considered a distinct improvement over petticoats because it weighed considerably less and did not constrict the wearer's legs as much.

Over the next decade, crinolines grew wider and wider—so wide that women wearing them could not fit through narrow doorways and gates, and a man escorting his wife could not get close enough to her to offer his arm. In addition, crinolines caused many embarrassing incidents; underclothes were often exposed when crinolines caught in a sudden wind gust blew up like balloons. Some incidents were not so funny. Women who moved too close to the fireplace would set their crinolines alight.

Charles Worth designed many dresses that required the crinoline, but he eventually came to dislike the garment and replaced it with other styles.

Worth slimmed dresses down, moving toward a narrow, flat front that followed the line of a woman's figure. By 1869, when the crinoline was fading out, Worth introduced the bustle, a round accessory made of horsehair petticoats and wire that a woman wore under her dress, near her lower back. In this way, Worth moved the fullness of skirts from the sides to the back, making it much easier for women to move freely.

Worth promoted technological advancement, using sewing machines and lace-making machines to help him produce 6,000 to 7,000 gowns each year.

A bustle from 1872

Experimenting with ways that fabric could be draped over a bustle, Worth created the fan train, which had three deep pleats at the top and spread out in a half-circle, like a fan, as it reached the floor. This fan train evening gown from 1873 was made of black gauze with gold stripes over black silk, with trimming of red, yellow, and black silk roses.

He also began using patterns made up of standardized parts. He had patterns for different bodices, skirts, and sleeves, and he would put together various combinations to create a dress. This made it easier for him to produce more dresses.

Worth's influence on fashion was so complete that the years during which he worked are often referred to as the Age of Worth. But in September 1870, when Prussia invaded France and the Second Empire collapsed, Worth was forced to close his doors. The empress fled France, and the French court system was replaced in 1871 by the Third Republic, headed by a president. Without his faithful court, this could have been the end of Worth's career, but by the mid-nineteenth century, the rise of banking and industry created by the Industrial Revolution had made many men newly wealthy. These men wanted their wives dressed by the best dressmaker in France: Charles Worth.

In March 1871, Worth reopened his fashion house to even greater success. His partner, Otto Bobergh, retired to Sweden, and the reopened design house became the House of Worth. In addition to his new French clients, Worth developed an international following. Unlike other dressmakers, who often disregarded the quality of the clothing they sent to their foreign customers, Worth provided the best quality clothing to his clients in the United States and South and Central America. Worth's customers became loyal clients, and he began providing patterns of his designs for reproduction overseas.

Worth continued to design and create new styles throughout the 1870s. He introduced the princess line, which consisted of dresses with fitted waists but no waist seams. This style was copied repeatedly by other designers. Worth branched out into other areas, designing elegant sportswear, mourning dresses, and maternity dresses. In 1874, his sons began working for their father full-time, Jean Philippe doing some designing and Gaston taking care of financial matters.

The 1891 Worth tea gown at left consisted of a long, flowing beige tunic over a close-fitting dress made of velvet stamped with a design in maroon. Worth's innovative "seamless" dress from 1892 (right) was an example of the princess line that he pioneered. Made of stretchy wool over a silk lining, it fastened invisibly on the left. The few seams that were necessary were concealed by trimming.

LEGACY

By the time Worth died at the age of 70 on March 10, 1895, he had racked up a long line of firsts in the fashion world—he was the first to use live models rather than dummies to show his clothes, the first to provide patterns of his designs, and the first to put his label on a dress. But most importantly, he was the first to be an actual fashion designer. No longer just dressmakers or tailors, designers now created fashions according to their own tastes and presented them to the public. Today, the garments that emerge from a couture house are valued as works of art by the women and men who buy them.

The House of Worth continued under Charles Worth's sons, Gaston and Jean Philippe, and then under their sons. The house introduced a line of perfumes in 1900. A great-grandson of Charles, Roger Worth, still headed Parfums Worth in 2002, although the design house was sold in 1946. The House of Worth closed its doors in 1956. But the prestige associated with a Worth original remains as solid as it was when Charles Worth dressed an empress and her court.

"[Worth] set the taste and ordained the fashion of Paris and from Paris extended his undisputed sway all over the civilized and a good deal of the uncivilized world. He knew how to dress woman as nobody else knew how to dress her."
—the *London Times*, after Worth's death

2

LEVI STRAUSS

"WAIST OVERALLS": FROM WORK GEAR TO HIGH FASHION

In 1906, the fires that followed a huge earthquake in San Francisco destroyed most of Levi Strauss & Co.'s records. A number of stories have since sprung up about the company's origins, and one of them goes like this: Immigrant Levi Strauss stepped off the boat he had taken to California, eager to begin his new life. He soon realized that the gold miners needed sturdier pants, so he made a pair out of some brown canvas he had brought with him. He later switched to using denim imported from France, thus inventing one of the most beloved modern fashions.

While this story is more legend than fact, the true story about Levi Strauss is the most fantastic one of all—he popularized and marketed the only

Levi Strauss (1829-1902), a Bavarian immigrant, created the most American of all fashions when he began manufacturing work pants known as "waist overalls."

39

clothing item created in the nineteenth century that was still being worn in the twenty-first: blue jeans.

A NEW LIFE IN AMERICA

Levi Strauss was born on February 26, 1829, in Buttenheim, a small town in Bavaria. (Bavaria is now a part of southern Germany.) Levi's parents, Hirsch and Rebecca Strauss, had two children together, Loeb (as Levi was originally named) and Fanny. Four children from Hirsch's first marriage made up the rest of the family. Hirsch earned a living peddling, or selling, dry goods.

dry goods: textiles, clothing and other related items

Life for the Jewish Strauss family was not easy while Loeb was growing up. Forced to live in a specific area of town called a ghetto, Jews faced many hardships and restrictions. For instance, they had to ask permission to marry, because the government wanted to keep the Jewish population from spreading beyond the confines of the ghetto.

In 1845, Hirsch Strauss contracted tuberculosis and died. Loeb's older half-brothers, Jonas and Louis, left the harsh conditions in Bavaria, hoping to find a better life for themselves in America. They settled in New York along with hundreds of other poor European immigrants who had the same dream of improving their prospects. The brothers set about building their new life by peddling goods on the streets of New York City. They were such successful salesmen that they soon opened their own dry-goods store, J. Strauss Brother & Co.

In 1847, Loeb (who was soon to be called Levi) traveled to New York with his mother and two sisters.

He started working in his brothers' store, learning the dry-goods business. Soon, he had learned enough to set out on his own. In 1848, a valuable business opportunity presented itself when big news spread across the United States: gold had been discovered in California. Stories of men becoming wealthy overnight fueled imaginations, and people across America caught gold fever. Thousands of men left their wives and children in the East in a mad rush to get to the California gold. News of the gold rush reached Levi Strauss, and he grew excited, too. All those men going to California would need to travel light and then buy most of their gear when they arrived. Among other things, the miners would need work clothes to wear and bedding for their camps. Strauss believed that selling these items was the way to make his fortune. He decided to set up his own dry-goods wholesale house in San Francisco, selling the supplies his brothers shipped to him from their business in New York.

wholesale house: a place that sells goods to retailers, usually in large quantities, for resale in their stores

SETTING UP SHOP

In March 1853, shortly after becoming an American citizen, Strauss arrived in the bustling city of San Francisco. He opened a wholesale house and called it simply "Levi Strauss." He chose a location near the docks to make it easier to receive the goods shipped to him from New York.

Selling supplies such as pillows, blankets, and underwear to the gold miners turned out to be very profitable. As his business expanded, Strauss had to move his wholesale house several times before finally settling in a large four-story complex on Battery Street. By 1856, his sister, Fanny, had moved to San Francisco with her husband, David Stern. Stern joined Strauss in his dry-goods business, now renamed Levi Strauss & Co. Strauss became known for providing goods of high quality, and he gained a reputation for treating his employees well. He even asked his workers to call him "Levi" instead of "Mr. Strauss."

In his spare time, Strauss pursued various interests besides his wholesale business. With the money he earned, he invested in real estate. He improved his properties and then sold them at a profit. He also became an avid philanthropist, helping to fund local Jewish schools and the synagogue he attended. Comfortable in the knowledge that he had accomplished his goal of building a successful life in America, Strauss had no idea that even greater success still lay ahead of him.

WAIST OVERALLS

When Strauss received a letter from one of his customers in July 1872, he became very excited. Jacob Davis, a tailor from Reno, Nevada, wrote to him with an interesting proposition. Davis had been buying fabric from Strauss and using it to make pants for laborers. The pockets of the pants he made had continually ripped off, so he began placing metal rivets at the points of strain—such as the corners of the pockets—to keep the pockets on the pants. Davis wanted to patent his invention so he would be able to market the pants without the risk of other

Jacob Davis in about 1900

tailors stealing his idea. But Davis could not afford $68 to apply for the patent. He asked Strauss to put up the money. In exchange for paying for the patent, Strauss would be allowed to sell the riveted pants. Strauss knew this idea would be a success, so he helped Davis patent his invention. The two received the patent for the riveted pants on May 20, 1873, and, at Strauss's invitation, Davis moved to San Francisco to oversee the manufacturing of their new product.

patent: government recognition that an invention belongs to a particular inventor, which gives the inventor the sole right to produce and sell the invention for the duration of the patent

Strauss and Davis's patent for their "improvement in fastening pocket-openings"

J. W. DAVIS.
Fastening Pocket-Openings.

No. 139,121.   Patented May 20, 1873.

Fig. 1.

Witnesses
J. L. Boone
E. H. Richardson

Inventor
Jacob W. Davis
per Dwight G.
Att'ys

UNITED STATES PATENT OFFICE.

JACOB W. DAVIS, OF RENO, NEVADA, ASSIGNOR TO HIMSELF AND LEVI STRAUSS & COMPANY, OF SAN FRANCISCO, CALIFORNIA.

IMPROVEMENT IN FASTENING POCKET-OPENINGS.

Specification forming part of Letters Patent No. 139,121, dated May 20, 1873; application filed August 9, 1872.

To all whom it may concern:

Be it known that I, JACOB W. DAVIS, of Reno, county of Washoe and State of Nevada, have invented an Improvement in Fastening Seams; and I do hereby declare the following description and accompanying drawing are sufficient to enable any person skilled in the art or science to which it most nearly appertains to make and use my said invention or improvement without further invention or experiment.

My invention relates to a fastening for pocket-openings, whereby the sewed seams are prevented from ripping or starting from frequent pressure or strain thereon; and it consists in the employment of a metal rivet or eyelet at each edge of the pocket-opening, to prevent the ripping of the seam at those points. The rivet or eyelet is so fastened in the seam as to bind the two parts of cloth which the seam unites together, so that it shall prevent the strain or pressure from coming upon the thread with which the seam is sewed.

In order to more fully illustrate and explain my invention, reference is had to the accompanying drawing, in which my invention is represented as applied to the pockets of a pair of pants.

Figure 1 is a view of my invention as applied to pants.

A is the side seam in a pair of pants, drawers, or other article of wearing apparel, which terminates at the pockets; and *b b* represent the rivets at each edge of the pocket opening. The seams are usually ripped or started by the placing of the hands in the pockets and the consequent pressure or strain upon them. To strengthen this part I employ a rivet, eyelet, or other equivalent metal stud, *b*, which I pass through a hole at the end of the seam, so as to bind the two parts of cloth together, and then bend it down upon both sides so as to firmly unite the two parts. When rivets which already have one head are used, it is only necessary to bend the opposite end, and a washer can be interposed, if desired, in the usual way. By this means I avoid a large amount of trouble in mending portions of seams which are subjected to constant strain.

I am aware that rivets have been used for securing seams in shoes, as shown in the patents to Geo. Houghton, No. 64,015, April 23, 1867, and to L. K. Washburn, No. 123,313, January 30, 1872; and hence I do not claim, broadly, fastening of seams by means of rivets.

Having thus described my invention, what I claim as new, and desire to secure by Letters Patent, is—

As a new article of manufacture, a pair of pantaloons having the pocket-openings secured at each edge by means of rivets, substantially in the manner described and shown, whereby the seams at the points named are prevented from ripping, as set forth.

In witness whereof I hereunto set my hand and seal.

JACOB W. DAVIS. [L. S.]

Witnesses:
JAMES O. HAGERMAN,
W. BERGMAN.

Strauss and Davis hired seamstresses who sewed the denim pants, or "waist overalls," as they were called, in their homes. As the demand for the waist overalls grew, Strauss and Davis had to find a more efficient system. They opened a factory, bringing the seamstresses together to make the pants. Each pair of pants was stitched with orange thread to match the copper rivets.

The denim waist overalls quickly gained a reputation for comfort and reliability. They became the unofficial uniform of California gold miners, who

One of Levi Strauss & Co.'s early waist overall factories, which employed more than 500 seamstresses

Miners dressed in waist overalls stand in front of a California mine in 1882.

liked the fact that the rivets kept their pockets from ripping under the weight of the ore samples they collected as they worked. In 1886, the company introduced a leather label, sewn onto the back of the pants, that symbolized their sturdiness. Showing two horses trying to pull apart a pair of pants, this label still adorns Levi Strauss & Co.'s products today.

Strauss's patent on the riveting process protected his business from competition by giving it the sole right to manufacture riveted clothing for nearly 20 years. When the patent expired around 1891, other

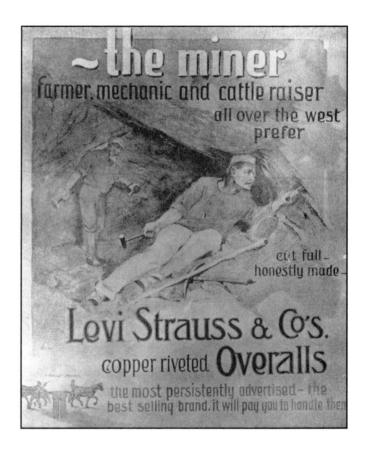

Even after other companies began to produce waist overalls, this 1905 Levi Strauss & Co. advertisement was able to claim "the best selling brand." The logo of two horses pulling at a pair of pants appears in the lower left corner.

companies rushed to imitate the unique pants he had popularized. But Strauss's products—Levi's, as they became known—remained the leading work pants of the West.

PASSING THE BUSINESS ON

The popularity of the waist overalls made Strauss wealthy beyond his dreams. When his company was officially incorporated in 1890, Strauss turned the running of the business over to his nephews, Jacob, Sigmund, Louis, and Abraham Stern (the sons of his

sister, Fanny). With the time to focus on other interests, Strauss sat on the board of directors of several
companies. He continued to purchase, improve, and
sell real estate, as well as contribute to Jewish schools
and other charities. For 12 years, Strauss watched as
his business grew under his nephews' guidance.

When Levi Strauss died peacefully at his home on
September 26, 1902, he left no sons and daughters of
his own, but his estate amounted to nearly $6 million.
His impact on San Francisco's business community

*The Levi Strauss & Co.
wholesale warehouse and
headquarters, with its
employees, in the 1880s*

The rising popularity of Levi's was demonstrated by this 1899 ad, which showed waist overalls being worn not only by miners, but also by railroad workers, carpenters, cowboys, and even children.

had been so great that many local shopowners closed their businesses to attend Strauss's funeral services.

LEGACY

Strauss's nephews kept Levi Strauss & Co. running profitably, and they would eventually pass it on to their children. After the earthquake of 1906, Strauss's nephews decided to do what Levi Strauss would have done and rebuilt the business. While rebuilding, they continued to pay their employees' wages and even extended loans to other, smaller businesses that had also suffered losses in the earthquake.

The status of Levi's waist overalls got a boost when Western movies became popular in the 1930s.

Levi's ads had an even more distinct Western theme by the 1940s.

Audiences saw movie stars such as John Wayne and Gary Cooper wearing Levi's while portraying cowboys. For many Americans, the West represented freedom and independence, and Levi's—as authentic Western gear—became a symbol of individualism. As Western ranches struggled to stay in business during the Great Depression, offering Western-style vacations became a popular way for them to bring in much-needed cash. Tourists often bought Levi's—which were not available in the East yet—on their trips out West and brought them home as souvenirs.

When Levi Strauss & Co. began to market its products across the United States in the 1950s, even more people discovered how comfortable they were, and pants made from denim fabric became increasingly prevalent. Teenagers in particular contributed to the continually rising popularity of denim pants, wearing Levi's as a symbol of rebellion. They also coined their own name for them—jeans (after a fabric similar to denim). Levi Strauss & Co. officially changed the name of its pants to jeans in 1960.

Levi Strauss's denim waist overalls have gone from being the dusty work pants of California gold miners to today's blue jeans—a uniquely American fashion worn by runway models and construction workers alike. Fashion designers such as Calvin Klein, Ralph Lauren, and Gloria Vanderbilt have created their own jeans with their labels on them (and almost all with metal rivets on them, as well). But Levi Strauss & Co. continues its reign as the most prominent name in jeans. Still owned by descendants of Levi Strauss, it is the world's largest

By the 1950s, jeans had progressed from work clothes to casual wear enjoyed by nearly all sections of society—including teenage girls (left). Designers soon reinvented jeans as high fashion with elaborate creations such as this 1971 denim vest-and-trouser outfit (right).

maker of brand-name clothing, with over $4 billion in sales in 2001. Its popular Levi's and Dockers brands are sold in more than 100 countries. But although the company designs jeans in many styles, the original Levi's—now made in more than 100 sizes and 20 different finishes and fabrics—remain its best-selling product.

The oldest existing pair of Levi's, made around 1890, were discovered in an abandoned silver mine in California's Mojave Desert in 1948. In 2001, they inspired a highly publicized bidding war when they were sold on the Internet site eBay. The winner, Levi Strauss & Co., bought the jeans for $46,532—the highest price ever paid for a piece of denim clothing— and placed them in its archives. The company produced a commemorative replica of the pants for sale to the public through its Vintage Clothing line.

Denim and Jean

The origins of the names of the fabrics used to make blue jeans are not clear. The name "denim" may come from a fabric that was woven in a French town called Nimes before the seventeenth century. While the denim we know today is woven from cotton, the Nimes fabric was a serge, or a blend of wool and a special kind of woolen yarn. It was very durable and was woven with one white thread and one colored thread. The French would have called the fabric *serge de Nimes*, which means "serge of (the town of) Nimes." Many scholars think that the word "denim" is an English corruption of the French phrase.

A different fabric made in Genoa, Italy, was called jean. Originally a fustian—a cotton, linen, and wool blend—jean was woven only from cotton by the eighteenth century.

Jean, although durable, was not as strong as denim, and, therefore, not as expensive. It was woven of two threads of the same color.

Both jean and denim were popular for making men's clothing. In nineteenth-century America, mechanics and painters wore blue denim overalls as workclothes. Jean was used to make slightly more tailored clothing, such as topcoats, vests, and short jackets, but "jeans pants" were also common. Although denim eventually gained greater popularity as a material for work pants, it appears the name "jeans" stuck, surviving long enough to be used by the teenage and college-age boys who became the major buyers of denim pants in the 1950s.

3

GABRIELLE "COCO" CHANEL

FASHION FOR THE MODERN WOMAN

Gabrielle Chanel loved the French resort town of Deauville, but on this trip, the wind was making her cold. She borrowed a polo player's warm but not very stylish sweater. She wrapped her own belt around the sweater and then pushed up the sleeves to make it fit. Then she decided to finish it off with a ribbon. As she looked over her handiwork, Chanel realized that the snazzy new sweater-jacket she had created would be perfect to sell in her Deauville shop, and she had some made up to sell. The "Chanel sweater" would help to propel Chanel into a designing career that would make her name known around the world for decades to come.

With her simple, elegant, and innovative styles, Gabrielle "Coco" Chanel (1883-1971) revolutionized women's fashion in the 1920s.

MODEST BEGINNINGS

Gabrielle Chanel was born in Saumur, France, on August 19, 1883. Her mother died of tuberculosis when Gabrielle was not quite 12 years old. Her father, Albert Chanel, placed Gabrielle and her two sisters in an orphanage in Aubazine and then disappeared. Gabrielle would never see her father again.

At the orphanage, Gabrielle slept in an unheated dormitory, separated from the girls whose relatives could afford to send at least some money. During the holidays, Gabrielle stayed with her grandparents and occasionally visited her aunt. At her aunt's house, she discovered romantic novels that introduced her to a world where everyone was rich, enjoyed a carefree existence, and wore beautiful clothes that were described in lavish detail. Gabrielle dreamed of escaping her hard life and climbing the social ladder to become like the characters in these books. When she turned 18, Gabrielle was sent from the orphanage to Notre Dame, a finishing school. The school agreed to take Gabrielle as a charity case, but she had to work in exchange for staying there.

After leaving Notre Dame in 1903, Gabrielle Chanel got a job in a lingerie and hosiery shop. She earned extra money by mending uniforms for the army officers stationed in town. At night, she sang in a cabaret. Even though Chanel was not a very good singer, she flirted with the officers and was quite popular. When a wealthy army officer named Etienne Balsan invited her to live at his country

finishing school: a private school that teaches young women how to run a household and behave correctly at social functions

cabaret: a nightclub that provides short programs of live entertainment

Chanel's nickname, Coco, may have been inspired by the songs she sang in the cabaret, particularly the popular hit "Qui-qu'a-vu-Coco."

estate in Compiègne, she believed this was her opportunity to create a new life for herself, and she accepted his invitation.

LIFE AT ROYALLIEU

The lifestyle at Balsan's estate, Royallieu, seemed to jump off the pages of Chanel's romance novels. Balsan invited groups of his friends to live at his estate for months at a time. The days and nights were filled with horseback riding, elegant dining, the opera, the theater, and parties. Chanel was surrounded by wealthy women who always dressed in the latest styles.

At the time, women's dresses were anything but comfortable. The ideal woman was supposed to have a large bust and hips, with a very small waist. Women achieved this look by wearing the popular S-bend corset, a rigid garment that slimmed and molded the wearer's waist, pushed her chest forward, and pressed her hips backward. Elaborate dresses made with yards of fabric and loads of trimmings—lace, ribbons, and bows—were draped over these corsets. Most wealthy women had a different costume for every activity and sometimes changed clothes (a task that required the help of several maids) as many as six times a day. Chanel thought her slim, almost boyish shape would look ridiculous in these styles.

Always independent and original, Chanel created her own look instead. She borrowed clothes from the men at Royallieu and restyled them so that they complemented her youthful figure. At a time when

Corsets were not only restrictive and uncomfortable, but they were also a health risk. Women often fainted because their corsets were laced so tightly they couldn't breathe well enough, and years of wearing corsets could gradually push their organs out of place. In addition, the sharp whalebone "stays" that made corsets stiff could pop out of the material and puncture the wearer's body, causing severe injury or even death.

The House of Chanel still resided at 31 Rue Cambon in 2002.

boutique: a small business offering specialized products or services, particularly a small retail store selling fashionable clothing

most women rode horses sidesaddle in long skirts, Chanel rode in breeches, men's pants that went down to the knee. She also began making simple hats with very little decoration—often only one feather plume. Chanel's hats contrasted sharply with the hats overloaded with trimmings that most other women wore. Some of the actresses Chanel knew from Royallieu were soon asking her to make hats for them. As her actress friends began telling others about her hats, Chanel thought of opening a millinery, or hat shop. She asked Etienne Balsan for help, and he allowed her to sell her hats out of his apartment in Paris.

BECOMING ESTABLISHED

Around 1910, while she was still at Royallieu, Chanel met and fell in love with a wealthy Englishman named Arthur "Boy" Capel. He encouraged her to open a millinery and even loaned her money to rent a location on the Rue Cambon, a street in the center of Paris's fashion district. Gossip about Chanel and Capel provided extra publicity for Chanel's new business, and many customers came to her shop out of curiosity about the unusual woman Boy Capel was dating. But even after they had satisfied their curiosity about Chanel, the women returned to her hat shop again and again. By the spring of 1913, Chanel was able to pay back all of Capel's loan.

That summer, with her Paris shop doing well, Chanel started a second boutique in the northern French resort town of Deauville. Again, Capel loaned her money to open the shop. For the first time, Chanel put her name on a storefront—her

Deauville shop sported a black awning with "Gabrielle Chanel" printed in white letters on the front. Chanel introduced informal knit and flannel resortwear to coordinate with her hats. She had had so many compliments on her own clothes that she simply created more like them and sold them in her boutique.

A LIBERATING STYLE FOR WOMEN

Chanel's emphasis on comfortable yet stylish clothes struck a chord with her customers. Sales of her resortwear took off. Although most of the Deauville shops closed during World War I, Chanel kept her boutique open. Many wealthy people fled to the resort town to escape the war, and women rushed to buy Chanel's clothes when her shop was the only one still doing business.

Women were also becoming more active than ever before. They were working in causes to support France in World War I, playing sports, and driving cars. For these activities, they needed clothing that allowed them to move easily, and Chanel's designs did just that. Her clothes made women feel comfortable and confident. The skirts were shorter than those of other designers and were cut more loosely, allowing the wearer to move easily. She also designed many outfits out of jersey—a soft, stretchy knit fabric. This was a daring move, since the material had previously been used only to make men's underwear, but Chanel loved how it molded softly to the shape of the wearer. One of her favorite looks consisted of a jersey jacket with pockets and

Soft, sporty jersey outfits in the style of Chanel remained popular with women throughout the 1920s.

turned-back cuffs, worn with a narrow belt and a matching skirt.

In 1915, Chanel and Capel vacationed in Biarritz, a beautiful resort near France's border with Spain. Like Deauville, Biarritz was filled with wealthy people looking for a place to avoid the war. On July 15, Chanel opened Biarritz's first fashion house—and her own first attempt at haute couture. The opening of the Biarritz store brought Chanel to the attention of American fashion magazines, which began to feature her designs. Chanel became the model of the new woman—short-haired, corsetless, and financially independent of men.

Then, in winter 1919, Capel was killed in a car accident. Chanel was devastated. She had her entire bedroom decorated in black, but then couldn't stand it and had to get out. She stayed dedicated to her business and bounced back, but she would never be the same without Capel. "I lost everything when I lost Capel. He left in me a void that the years have not fulfilled," she later said.

Costume Design

Through her friendships with actors, playwrights, and artists, Chanel eventually began designing theatrical costumes. In 1922, Chanel's friend Jean Cocteau organized and directed an interpretation of *Antigone*, a play by the ancient Greek playwright Sophocles. Painter Pablo Picasso designed the sets, and Cocteau asked Chanel to do the costumes. Though many viewers found Cocteau's experimental version of the play disconcerting, Chanel's costumes were a hit. She was invited to design costumes for other plays, including ballet productions by her friends Serge Diaghilev and Igor Stravinsky.

Another of Chanel's friends introduced her to Samuel Goldwyn, an American moviemaker. Goldwyn asked Chanel to design costumes for some of his upcoming movies, hoping to draw more people to his films with Chanel's fame. Chanel hesitated at first, but when Goldwyn offered her $1 million for one year of designing, she agreed.

In 1931, Chanel flew to Hollywood. Her costume designs were not the glittery eveningwear-worn-as-daywear clothes of previous screen designers. She clothed famous actresses such as Gloria Swanson in classic, simple suits—clothes a woman could wear offstage. Her designs weren't sensational enough, and the four movies she designed for brought her little publicity. Chanel returned to her Paris couture business by the end of the year, but she continued to design costumes for European art-film directors such as Jean Renoir. Chanel also dressed international film stars, including Romy Schneider, Lauren Bacall, Greta Garbo, and Marlene Dietrich.

Chanel with Dimitri Pavlovich

Chanel's style in jewelry was as creative as her hats and clothing. She was the first designer to create fashionable costume jewelry, using glass stones and fake pearls instead of precious gems.

INFLUENTIAL RELATIONSHIPS

In 1920, Chanel became romantically involved with the Grand Duke Dimitri Pavlovich. A cousin of the late Russian tsar, Pavlovich was in exile from Russia due to the Communist revolution of 1917. He introduced Chanel to traditional designs from his country, and her dresses quickly acquired a distinct Russian peasant style. Chanel hired Dimitri's sister, who was also in exile, to head a workroom that would produce vividly colored Russian embroidery. Pavlovich also lavished his Russian jewels on Chanel, inspiring her to create her own line of costume jewelry in the mid-1920s.

Chanel was not one to be tied to one man for too long. She soon parted ways with Pavlovich and in 1925 became involved with one of Britain's wealthiest men, the duke of Westminster. Through him, she met the Prince of Wales and Winston Churchill, who would later become England's prime minister. Chanel was the first designer—still just a dressmaker to many people—to be so accepted in aristocratic society.

Just as her relationship with Dimitri had introduced Russian elements into her designs, Chanel's

Chanel attends Britain's Grand National horse race with the duke of Westminster (1879-1953) in 1925. The duke's full name was Hugh Richard Arthur Grosvenor, but he was known to friends as "Bendor."

relationship with the duke of Westminster introduced elements of British dress. Her new designs incorporated striped waistcoats from the uniforms of the duke's servants, berets and sailor collars from yachting cruises, and tweed from Scotland. She added fur to tweed coats to create a softer, more feminine look. She also designed cardigans along the lines of Scottish Fair Isle sweaters, with their distinct bands of geometric patterns.

CHANEL NO. 5

In 1920, through Dimitri Pavlovich, Chanel met another man who would influence the course of her future: Ernest Beaux, who had been the Russian tsar's chemist before the Communist takeover. Chanel wanted to create a fragrance, and Beaux was just the person to help her. Chanel asked Beaux to invent a scent for her—something totally different than anything on the market at the time. The current perfumes all smelled very flowery and, to Chanel, artificial. She believed that enhancing the natural perfumes with synthetic blends would produce a more natural smell. It worked. Beaux used a jasmine base and added a man-made chemical to make the scent stronger and longer-lasting.

Chanel introduced her perfume in 1921. Chanel No. 5 not only smelled more natural than other perfumes, but it also had a simpler name and bottle. Most other perfumes were named after flowers and came in elaborate, ornate bottles. Chanel attached her name to her perfume—the first time a designer had ever done this—and designed a simple square

Madame Gabrielle Chanel in her new apartment in the Ritz, Paris

Photo by Kollar, courtesy Harper's Bazaar

Madame Gabrielle Chanel is above all an artist in living. Her dresses, her perfumes, are created with a faultless instinct for drama. Her Perfume No. 5 is like the soft music that underlies the playing of a love scene. It kindles the imagination; indelibly fixes the scene in the memories of the players.

LES PARFUMS

CHANEL

GLAMOUR de CHANEL   GARDENIA de CHANEL   CUIR de RUSSIE (Russia Leather)

No.5 CHANEL

A 1937 advertisement for Chanel No. 5, featuring a picture of Gabrielle Chanel. Chanel created four other fragrances with Ernest Beaux between 1922 and 1927: No. 22, Gardenia, Bois des Iles, and Cuir de Russie. She also launched a line of skin-care and make-up products, and in 1924 she founded Les Parfums Chanel to distribute her perfumes and cosmetics throughout the world.

bottle with a square stopper. She gave little bottles of the scent to special friends, making them feel privileged to wear it, and sprayed the perfume in all her boutiques. Chanel No. 5 went on to become the most successful part of Chanel's business.

LONG-LASTING DESIGNS

Chanel created a number of designs that are still considered classics. She introduced one of her most famous, the Chanel suit, in 1925. Typically made of

The mystery surrounding Chanel's choice of the number five for the name of her perfume enhanced its appeal. Some thought five was Chanel's lucky number; others claimed Ernest Beaux had made more than one scent for Chanel to try—and she chose number five.

"A Chanel suit is made for a woman who moves," said Gabrielle Chanel, shown here wearing one of her own creations in 1929.

jersey, the suit consisted of a "collarless, braid-trimmed cardigan jacket with long, tight-fitting sleeves" and a matching knee-length skirt. The jacket featured slightly padded shoulders and two patch pockets. A crisp white blouse finished it off. Chanel could often be seen wearing an off-white version of this suit, with navy blue trim, loaded with bunches of her signature costume jewelry. This suit, according to one of Chanel's biographers, "would be more copied, in all price ranges, than any other single garment designed by a couturier."

Schiaparelli

Chanel's biggest rival during the 1930s was an Italian designer named Elsa Schiaparelli (1896-1973). Schiaparelli started out designing sweaters with geometric patterns reminiscent of the cubist art popular at the time. After she opened her own Paris couture house, her designs became more and more outrageous as she incorporated surrealist art into them. She enlisted the help of artist Salvador Dali to create a dress printed with a huge lobster on the skirt and a splash of green on the bodice to represent parsley. Schiaparelli also loved using wild colors, such as her trademark "shocking pink."

Schiaparelli's accessories were just as outrageous as her clothing designs. She designed a hat with a shoe on it and one shaped like a slab of beef. She produced black gloves with red fingernails painted on them and handbags that lit up or played songs. She used buttons shaped like everything but buttons and used padlocks as belt closures. Schiaparelli also inspired a military look that would be worn throughout World War II, designing jackets with square, padded shoulders for her suits.

Even though many of her designs were outlandish, Schiaparelli's clothes had the same crisp and clean feel as Chanel's, and she appealed to the same kind of customer. The two women often sent verbal barbs each other's way. When Chanel said, "What I make is picked up and copied by everybody," Schiaparelli replied, "What I create is inimitable." Schiaparelli closed her couture house in 1950.

A drawing of Chanel in her little black dress of 1926, as imagined by Karl Lagerfeld (head designer of the House of Chanel since 1983)

Another of Chanel's classic designs was her "little black dress." In the middle of the 1920s, an era of glitz, sparkle, and bold colors, Chanel introduced simple, comfortable black dresses for day or evening. Her black dress for daytime was a long-sleeved chemise made of wool, while her black evening dresses were made from either lace, silk, satin, or velvet. In 1926, *Vogue* magazine compared Chanel's black dress to the Ford car, implying that it would "become standard wear for the masses"—and it did. It has since become a cliché that every fashionable woman must have a little black dress in her closet.

In 1932, Chanel launched a collection of fine jewelry in diamonds and platinum. It was a daring move to introduce such expensive products during the Great Depression, but Chanel's simple, versatile designs again proved a great success. Her jewelry could be worn in the daytime as well as in the evening. Some pieces were even convertible; one long necklace could be taken apart and worn separately as a brooch and a short necklace.

RETIREMENT AND COMEBACK

When the German army entered Poland in 1939 and France declared war on Germany, Chanel, like many other fashion designers, closed the doors of

"I started creating costume jewelry because I felt it was refreshingly free of arrogance, during a period that tended toward ostentatious displays of luxury. This consideration faded away into the background during the economic recession, when in every sphere of life, there emerged an instinctive desire for authenticity."
—Gabrielle Chanel, on her reasons for creating a fine jewelry collection in 1932

The "Comet" necklace was the most famous piece from Chanel's 1932 jewelry collection. Made of 600 diamonds with a total weight of 70 carats, it took nine months to make. It was carefully designed to bend between every two diamonds so that it wrapped flexibly around the wearer's neck. The House of Chanel re-created the Comet necklace in 1993 to launch its Fine Jewelry Boutique.

Business boomed at Chanel's boutique on the Rue Cambon when Paris was liberated from the Nazis at the end of World War II in 1945. American soldiers lined up in front of the store, eager to buy some of the famous Chanel No. 5 perfume to take home for their wives, girlfriends, mothers, and sisters.

her couture business, continuing to sell only her perfumes and accessories. In 1940, the German army marched into Paris. More than two million people, including Chanel, fled the city. During the war, Chanel lived in seclusion in Switzerland, returning to Paris only for brief visits.

In 1947, when Christian Dior's "New Look" took over the fashion world with its tiny waists and whalebone bodices reminiscent of the 1890s, Chanel was appalled. Male designers had begun to dominate the French couture business, and Chanel lashed out at their restrictive designs: "Fashion has become a

joke; the designers have forgotten that there are women inside the dresses. Most women dress for men and want to be admired. But they must also be able to move, to get into a car without bursting their seams! Clothes must have a natural shape." She attacked Dior specifically, saying that he "doesn't dress women, he drapes them." Someone had to do something, Chanel thought.

On February 5, 1954, Chanel launched a comeback collection. Models paraded by in her trademark jersey suits in dark colors and feminine, softly draping jersey dresses. French fashion critics attacked the collection, calling it "a fiasco," "a collection for mothers," and a collection of "ghosts of 1930," but the American fashion world still appreciated Chanel's simplicity. *Life* magazine did a four-page spread on her, and *Vogue* featured her clothes on its next cover. By the time she presented her third show after her comeback, Chanel was again firmly established, even with the French critics.

Throughout the 1960s, when clothes became bright and bold and focused on youth, Chanel continued designing clothes in the same tradition she always had. She criticized older women for wanting to dress like teenagers and berated the trendy miniskirt as "gaudy and indecent." Chanel's stylish, yet comfortable and simple, clothing remained popular despite the trends, and Chanel continued designing into her eighties. Her signature elements during this time included braid-trimmed tweed suits, light-colored slingback shoes with black toes, and shoulder bags with plaited leather straps.

In 1957, Chanel was honored with the prestigious Neiman Marcus Award for Distinguished Service in the Field of Fashion, also known as the "fashion Oscar." Here, she poses aboard an airplane on her way to the United States to receive the award.

LEGACY

When she died in 1971, Chanel had become a leading couturier whose designs passed from mothers to their daughters. Her suits, little black dresses, and jewelry remained as popular as they were when she first combined comfort and style for the woman of the 1920s. Chanel's early designs reflected women's emerging independence as they became active in wartime efforts, took on professional careers, and gained the right to vote. Even more successful than her couture, her perfumes continue to symbolize simplicity and elegance.

The House of Chanel continued under the guidance of Karl Lagerfeld, who became head designer in 1983. The design house needed someone to help it regain its place as a leading Paris fashion house. The Chanel suit was associated with an older clientele, but Lagerfeld reinvented it and other Chanel trademarks in clever ways that appealed to an entirely new audience. He added Coco Chanel's famous double "C" insignia to motorcycle boots and leggings to give the Chanel trademark a younger, sportier feel. He retained the distinctive loose, square jacket and skirt of the traditional Chanel suits but changed them in ways that added a bit of fun to the design. His designs attracted younger women without alienating Chanel's established clientele. With more than 200 boutiques around the world, the House of Chanel continues to produce quality couture garments for women who demand comfort as well as style in the twenty-first century.

"Fashion is not something that exists in dresses only; fashion is something in the air. It's the wind that blows in the new fashion; you feel it coming, you smell it. Fashion is in the sky, in the street, fashion has to do with ideas, the way we live, what is happening."
—Gabrielle Chanel

The House of Chanel is a private company controlled by chairman Alain Wertheimer and his family. Although it rarely releases its financial information, sales in 1995 were estimated at more than $1 billion. Karl Lagerfeld has stated that when he came to Chanel, fashion made up only 6 percent of the company's total sales. Since then, he says, it has grown to more than 50 percent.

Karl Lagerfeld (b. 1938),
shown at left, designs couture, ready-to-wear, and
accessories for the House of
Chanel. Below, Stella
Tennant models part of his
Chanel 2002 spring/summer
ready-to-wear collection.

4

CHRISTIAN DIOR

THE NEW LOOK

On a street in Paris in 1947, two fashionably dressed women stood talking. They didn't notice the group of women moving toward them until it was too late. One member of the group swung her purse, and the two realized they were under attack. They screamed, but it was no use—in minutes they were surrounded by an angry mob intent on ripping their new Dior dresses to shreds. When a picture of the incident was splashed across newspapers worldwide, Christian Dior knew he had touched a nerve with his "New Look." Dior's wide skirts made of yards and yards of fabric and his nineteenth-century-style dresses, complete with corsets, had made some people angry.

Christian Dior's career as an independent designer with his own couture house lasted only 10 years. But in that decade, he turned the fashion world upside

Christian Dior (1905-1957) uses a tape measure to demonstrate the longer skirt lengths he initiated with his controversial "New Look" for women's fashion.

down. Rejecting the short skirts and square jackets of the World War II years, which he considered unflattering, Dior introduced a dramatic change in style that redefined women's fashion in the postwar era.

EARLY DESIGNING

Christian Dior was born on January 21, 1905, in Granville, France, where his father, Alexandre Louis Maurice Dior, owned a fertilizer factory. As a child, Christian loved to sketch costumes for himself and his brothers and sisters to wear to Granville's yearly festival, Carnival. He watched eagerly as Juliette, the

At the age of two, Christian Dior (left) stands with his mother and brother outside "Les Rhumbs," their home in Granville. The house became the Christian Dior Museum in 1997.

family's seamstress, brought his sketches to life on the sewing machine. Christian's designs were always elaborate. One year he designed a King Neptune costume for his sister, with a shell-covered bodice and a skirt made from the leaves of a raffia palm tree.

Christian knew early on that he wanted to study art, and he hoped his parents would let him attend the Academy of Fine Arts in Paris. They, however, were very much against this—art was not considered a suitable career for someone of Christian's social standing. To please his parents, Christian attended the School of Political Science in Paris, but he stayed connected to the art scene through his many artist friends. Christian loved coming up with costumes for the plays they staged. He paid special attention to every detail of the costumes. But even though Christian was enjoying going to parties with his friends, he knew he needed to decide on a career.

In 1925, Christian met the couturier Paul Poiret, who had been the first to design women's dresses with a more relaxed corset. Poiret considered himself an artist rather than simply a designer of clothes, which intrigued Christian. Still, Christian knew his parents would never approve if he pursued a similar career, so, with their grudging permission, he opened an art gallery instead.

Losing Everything

The Dior family fortunes changed drastically in the early 1930s. In 1931, Christian's mother died. Then Christian's father lost all of the family's money in land speculation. He had borrowed money in 1929

Carnival, Granville's annual party with elaborate costumes and parades, grew out of the town's position on the Atlantic coast. Sailors would celebrate in mid-February before going off to a cold and lonely life at sea. Carnival later developed into a celebration of the last days before Lent, the Catholic period of fasting and self-denial before Easter. When Granville became a resort town, Carnival lengthened into a summer-long festival put on mainly for tourists.

Paul Poiret (1879-1944) designed for the House of Worth before starting his own business. His "hobble" skirts—long skirts that narrowed below the knees— became a popular fashion in the 1910s.

to develop a piece of land he owned, but that same year the United States stock market crashed, and thousands of Americans lost all of the money they had. By 1931, France was feeling the effects of the crash, and Maurice Dior's stocks had dropped drastically in value. He could not repay his loans.

Christian's art gallery had to be closed. He was now penniless, although he continued to attend and throw spectacular parties with his friends. In 1934, Christian contracted tuberculosis, and his friends arranged for him to spend a year recuperating on Ibiza, an island off the eastern coast of Spain. While on the island, he became interested in tapestry weaving, one of the local handicrafts. Once again, he was creating artistic designs, and he had never felt happier. He knew that whatever he did in the future would have to involve this kind of self-expression.

After his illness, Christian returned to Paris to help his now-destitute father and sister, but he could not find a job. After being turned down for an office position at a fashion design house, Christian began to give serious thought to becoming a couturier, but he struggled with the decision. His experience on Ibiza had given him another glimpse of the pleasure he received from creating things, but with the exception of Gabrielle Chanel—who had managed to be accepted in the highest levels of society—couturiers were considered tradesmen.

TAKING THE PLUNGE

Christian Dior finally decided to pursue what he loved. He realized how much he had loved designing costumes for Carnival and the plays he staged with his friends. To earn enough money to get started, he sold a painting he had bought from Paul Poiret. Jean Ozenne, a fashion illustrator, invited Dior to live with him to save on living expenses. Ozenne encouraged Dior to become a fashion illustrator and gave him advice about getting started. Dior worked hard at learning to illustrate, and he was ecstatic when he sold six illustrations of his own. The sale of these drawings gave him the confidence he needed to pursue his dream wholeheartedly. He began designing both hats and dresses. Magazines, milliners, and garment manufacturers bought his designs, and soon he earned enough money to move into his own apartment.

Then Dior met the couturier Robert Piguet. Not only did Piguet buy some of Dior's designs, but he also asked Dior to design dresses for his next show. These designs were so successful that, in 1938, Piguet hired Dior as a full-time designer. At last, Dior was able to make his creations come alive in fabrics, rather than simply drawing them on paper.

In 1939, just as Dior was beginning to feel comfortable in his new profession, France declared war on Germany. (Germany, under Adolf Hitler and the Nazis, had previously been threatening to take over much of Europe and had just begun to do so by invading Poland.) Dior was called to military service and given the unusual assignment of assisting women whose farmer husbands had gone to war. He came to love the peaceful routine of his farming duties.

"I was particularly struck by the interest and intense concentration with which this young designer went about his task. This fellow was maniacal in his detail, giving extremely precise instructions and leaving no room for interpretation."
—Denise Tual, whose husband, Roland, directed a 1939 play for which Christian Dior designed the costumes

Once his time in the service was over, Dior went to live with his father and sister in a small cottage in Provence. Dior busied himself with transforming the flower garden into a vegetable garden. He might have chosen to remain a farmer, but the fashion industry in Paris had not forgotten his talents as a designer.

In June 1941, Robert Piguet asked Dior to come back to his old job. Dior thought about it for a while, and, at the end of autumn, he returned to Paris. Unfortunately, Piguet had already hired someone else. But Dior received another offer— from Lucien Lelong, a couturier who dressed some of France's most elegant ladies. Dior accepted and went to work for Lelong.

THE HOUSE OF DIOR

Three years later, a wealthy Frenchman named Marcel Boussac decided that he wanted to reopen an old couture house and would finance the right designer to head it. An old childhood friend of Christian Dior was helping Boussac look for a designer. The friend happened to run into Dior on the street several times and kept asking him whether he could suggest anyone for the job. At first, Dior said he could think of no one. But by the third meeting, Dior felt fate had intervened, and he said he was interested himself. After looking at the setup of the couture house Boussac was renovating, Dior felt sure he did not want to reopen an old couture house. Instead, he proposed that Boussac finance the opening of a brand new one: the House of Dior.

Christian Dior negotiated an advantageous contract with Marcel Boussac. Dior would receive one-third of the profits in addition to his salary, and, most importantly, he would be head of the company—meaning he would make all final decisions regarding the House of Dior.

Dior had been considering opening his own house for a while, but he needed financial backing and encouragement. He dreamed of designing clothes for the "new" woman. During the war, fashions had become very conservative and even dowdy. Colors were dull, and styles were limited because fabric was rationed. Dior was certain that women wanted to look elegant and fashionable again, and he was eager to design clothes that would accomplish this. Inspired by Dior's dream, Boussac agreed to finance the project.

Christian Dior fought hard to acquire the right location for his couture house. By December 16, 1946, the House of Dior officially resided right where Dior had wanted it—at 30 Avenue Montaigne in Paris—and it has remained there ever since.

Utility Clothing

The fashion industry suffered during World War II (1939-1945). The Nazi occupation of France cut off Paris from the rest of the world and caused many designers to close their couture houses. New clothing was in short supply as fabric and manufacturing plants were diverted to the war effort. In 1941, Great Britain instituted clothes rationing and the Utility scheme—a government program to control the quality and price of clothing. In 1942, maximums in width and length of skirts were established, and pleats (which required extra fabric) were restricted.

Limited by these rules and inspired by military styles, women's clothing became regimented and straight. Jackets had squared shoulders and fewer buttons, while skirts were straight and fell to the knee or slightly below. This type of clothing became known as Utility clothing, and it spread throughout Britain, France, and the United States. Christian Dior, working at Lucien Lelong at the time, didn't like anything about the wartime styles. "Hats were far too large, skirts far too short, jackets far too long, [and] shoes far too heavy," he later said.

In Britain, rationing lasted until 1949 and the Utility scheme until 1952. Dior wanted the designs he introduced to be a relief from "a poverty-stricken, parsimonious era, obsessed with ration books and clothes coupons."

Excited and nervous about opening his own couture house, Dior left Lelong in December 1946 and went to the country to prepare his new designs. He spent two weeks sketching before he found his "spark"—the single idea around which he would design his collection. Then he locked himself away in his room, sketching furiously. He rested for a few days before putting together his final drawings. From these sketches, toiles—canvas models of the dresses—were made by his seamstresses. The toiles allowed Dior to see how well the design worked and whether his seamstresses had correctly expressed his vision. Next, the actual dresses were made. Then

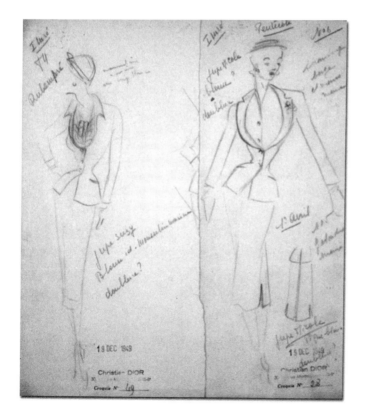

Some original sketches of clothing ideas by Christian Dior

Dior drapes fabric over a model while planning a new creation.

came preliminary fittings in which real models wore the dresses, which were checked for proper drape and fit. Then Dior added or changed the details, including hats, buttons, and bows. The dresses were often named at this stage of the process. Once Dior was satisfied with the clothes, he staged rehearsals for the fashion show. As the models strode past him, he watched carefully, noticing which dresses caught his eye. These would be the signature pieces that defined the collection. Dior would follow the same method when designing his future collections.

THE NEW LOOK

A few days before the opening of his fashion house, Dior gave a private showing of his dresses for a few friends. Their excitement spread through Paris, and when the show opened on February 12, 1947, the audience was stunned.

Dior's collection exaggerated the female shape. He introduced two main lines, one known as "En Huit," meaning "figure eight," and another called "Corolla," after the folded petals of a flower. Bodices were tight; waists were squeezed in by corsets. Long,

The "Diorama" dress, part of the Corolla line of Dior's fall/winter 1947 collection, helped introduce the small-waisted, large-skirted look that became his trademark.

full skirts that used yards of material blossomed in wide arcs. Flirty and frilly, Dior's dresses were very different from the square jackets and straight, short skirts that women had been wearing. One woman declared, "We are saved, becoming clothes are back, gone the stern padded shoulders, in are soft rounded shoulders without padding, nipped in waists, wide, wide skirts about four inches below the knee." A prominent American fashion editor, Carmel Snow, took one glance at the collection and announced that Dior had given women a "new look." This name quickly took hold and was forever associated with Dior's clothing, especially the first collection.

The "Bar" suit was the signature design in Dior's first collection. The jacket was made of cream-colored shantung—a heavy, rough fabric made of spun wild silk—and had a peplum (an overskirt or ruffle at the waist) to emphasize the female form. The black wool skirt had deep pleats that made it flare as the wearer walked.

Wealthy women rushed out to buy the New Look, and even women who could not afford the original designs were excited about it. The New Look expressed what many people were feeling. After the hardships and sacrifices of Paris's difficult war years, they wanted to move ahead with their lives and look toward a more positive future.

Even French garment manufacturers, who had previously made only conservative, unoriginal clothing, began copying the New Look. It was the first time the mass market in France had followed haute couture. But Dior really knew his New Look was a success when all the most important American department stores—such as Bendel, Marshall Fields, and Bloomingdale's—ordered it. The House of Dior quickly expanded, adding two more workrooms and another building to its premises in the first year.

Dior's New Look was popular, but not everyone embraced it. After the ravages of World War II, economic depression had affected many European countries, and Britain and France continued to ration clothes. Some people thought that Dior was being insensitive by using so much material to make one dress when people were still struggling just to buy food. The tightly corseted waistline also angered some women because they felt it was a step backward. Women had spent years in the nineteenth and early twentieth centuries fighting to be allowed an education, to work outside the home, and to win the right to vote. Dior's traditionally feminine dresses seemed to place women in the position of being little more than decoration for men.

"We came from an epoch of war and uniforms, with women like soldiers with boxers' shoulders. I designed flower women, soft shoulders, full busts, waists as narrow as lianas [tropical vines], and skirts as corollas."
—Christian Dior

In the United States, opposition to Dior's New Look was more organized than in Europe. A Georgia woman founded the Just Below the Knee Club to dictate skirt lengths after she caught her ankle-length New Look skirt in the door of a bus and was dragged a block. Men formed the League of Broke Husbands to oppose Dior's use of so much expensive fabric—an average of 20 yards of material per dress, at a time when conventional outfits used 3 yards.

The "Schumann" ballgown, part of Dior's spring/summer 1950 collection, typified the flowery, flowing look that attracted some people and angered others.

CONQUERING AMERICA

In 1947, Neiman Marcus (the largest deluxe department store in the United States) invited Dior to the U.S. to receive its "fashion Oscar," the Award for Distinguished Service in the Field of Fashion. On his arrival in America, Dior was met by angry men and women who claimed that his dresses enslaved women to their clothes because the whalebone corsets, wide hats, and huge skirts restricted movement. Dior loved the controversy, since it gave him free publicity. "The battle of the New Look is all the rage," he said. "I don't think our name has ever been as widely known as now." The House of Dior rocketed to the top of the fashion scene.

Dior returned to Paris with plans to expand into the American market. He showed his first collection designed specifically for Americans in November 1948. Sized somewhat larger than their French counterparts, the dresses were available with modifications that allowed them to be worn in different climates. The critics gave the line rave reviews. In Paris, Dior was a designer of haute couture, but in America, he became known as a designer of deluxe ready-to-wear. Dior succeeded in the United States because he studied how the American fashion industry operated. Dior priced his line similar to other deluxe American collections, and he respected American work practices, but he did not sacrifice control over the designs—the House of Dior ran the American company.

DIOR WORLDWIDE

The House of Dior expanded rapidly into other markets, and Dior's name began showing up all over the place. He had considered creating a perfume even before the fashion house opened, and, in October 1948, the "Miss Dior" fragrance was introduced. In 1949, Dior began a string of licensing deals. He was the first designer to develop licenses for accessories, and he did so in almost every area of fashion—hosiery, furs, ties, handbags, gloves, jewelry, and hats. Dior was still responsible for these designs, but he licensed others to manufacture and distribute

In 1955, Dior posed for this picture surrounded by some of the accessories he designed and licensed—including hats, gloves, lingerie, purses, and jewelry.

the finished products. He was able to maintain complete control over production and marketing while charging the licensee a hefty fee for the use of the Dior name. In 1952, knowing that people were copying his designs, he began selling patterns to manufacturers and allowing them to place the Dior label on their finished garments. This way, he even earned money from reproductions of his garments.

SHAPES AND SILHOUETTES

Christian Dior's creations were inspired by shapes. Until 1954, his clothing designs were all based on some variation of his original flower silhouette. When he felt he had exhausted this look, he began playing with others. He produced different shapes every season, each one flatter and longer in the torso than the last. In August 1954, he created the H line, with the A and Y lines following in 1955. The dresses looked like the letter for which they were named. For example, the H line flattened the bust and gave women a streamlined, straight shape that Carmel Snow christened the "Flat Look." (Poorly received by the public, the H line also became known as the "string-bean look.") The Y-line dress

These 1954 coats illustrate some of the silhouettes popularized by Dior and soon imitated by his rivals. On the right is a Dior H-line coat; the other two, by different designers, represent the A (left) and S lines.

was very narrow at the waist with a tight skirt reaching to just below the knee. A short bolero-like jacket gave the width that formed the top of the Y. In 1957, Dior presented the "Free Line," which had hemlines that were much higher than his original New Look. Just a few months later, at age 52, Christian Dior died suddenly from a heart attack.

LEGACY

Christian Dior revolutionized the world of fashion with his New Look. Although some fierce opposition to the clothes surfaced, the look spread like wildfire all over the world. As the first to license his name, Dior created a strategy that many designers have since taken advantage of. Dior also started the practice of selling patterns to manufacturers, which meant that women who could not afford his original designs could still buy Dior by Bendel or Bloomingdale's.

The House of Dior achieved more than $12 billion in sales in 2001. Most of its profits stem from its 43 percent share in Louis Vuitton-Möet Hennessy (LVMH), a huge luxury fashion conglomerate. LVMH makes wines, champagnes, and cognacs; perfumes; cosmetics; fashion (including Givenchy and Donna Karan); luggage and other leather goods; and watches and jewelry. Both LVMH and Christian Dior are controlled by the same man, Bernard Arnault.

The House of Dior's reputation remained intact under Dior's successors. First, from 1957 to 1960, was Yves Saint Laurent, a famous designer in his own right. Marc Bohan took over for the next 29 years, and then Gianfranco Ferre served as chief designer from 1989 until 1996. Then came John Galliano, who arrived at Dior after heading Givenchy, another prominent fashion company, for more than a year. Galliano was the first British designer to head an established French couture house.

Dior's mother might have been appalled at seeing the family name on the front of a store, but in the fashion industry, the Dior name has been everywhere, always representing the very best in fashion.

Sales of women's ready-to-wear clothing increased fourfold at the House of Dior after popular designer John Galliano (above) came to the company in 1996. At right is one of Galliano's designs, the "Princess Afsharid" suit, from the Dior fall/winter 1997-1998 haute couture collection.

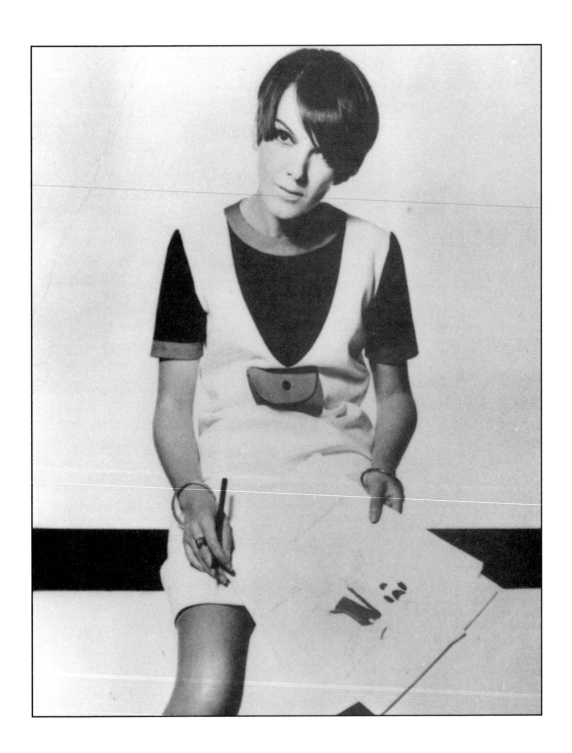

5

MARY QUANT

THE CHELSEA GIRL AND THE MOD LOOK

The lights dimmed, and the audience members raised their eyes expectantly. The first model posed at the top of a wide staircase, and the sounds of classical music floated through the ballroom of the Palace Hotel in St. Moritz, Switzerland. The room was full of fashion writers and clothing store buyers. All at once, the music switched to jazz, and the model suddenly dashed down the stairs, dancing before the audience. Shocked, the viewers barely had enough time to recover as model after model flew down the stairs, crossed the ballroom, swirled quickly, and then disappeared. The effect was electrifying. Never before had this audience, filled with members of the fashion elite, had a collection like this one presented to them. Instead of the silks and

An unconventional approach to both fashion and business made Mary Quant (b. 1934) one of the most influential designers of the swinging '60s.

minks they had been expecting, they saw an array of short flannel dresses and brightly colored stockings worn with boots.

The designer behind the radically new fashion show was Mary Quant, and her entire approach to fashion had the same madcap feel about it. Quant was the first to design clothes specifically for young people. She was also a force behind the hugely influential Chelsea movement, a cultural change that took over London and spread throughout the world in the late 1950s and early 1960s. By selling her original designs in small, trendy boutiques, Quant changed the way clothing was marketed to the public. Creative and inexpensive, her clothes appealed to a different audience than that of traditional haute couture. For the first time, fashion trends were initiated by young people of average means, rather than by wealthy, upper-class men and women.

REDHEADS SHOULD WEAR GREEN

Mary Quant's Welsh parents, Jack and Mildred, were both teachers. She was born on February 11, 1934, in a London suburb called Blackheath. As a young girl, Mary hated learning the fashion "rules" from her mother: redheads like Mary should always wear green, and accessories such as shoes, purses, and gloves should always match. Mary asked her mother why, but, she said, "No one ever gave me a satisfactory answer." She dreamed of the day when she would be able to wear anything she wanted, instead of the conservative dresses handed down to her by her cousin.

"I decided that such rules were totally irrelevant to modern-day living. Rules are invented for lazy people who don't want to think for themselves."
—Mary Quant

Mary began designing her own clothes by remaking her cousin's dresses into more contemporary styles. One time she made a school outfit—with a short, flared skirt and boys' white knee socks—that made all the other girls at school jealous. (She got away with wearing it because she said it was her uniform at her last school.) "I knew clothes would be the great interest of my life," she remembered. "But

Mary Quant's fascination with design and fabrics began early, as she later recalled: "When I was about six and in bed with measles, I spent one night cutting up a bedspread—a sort of family heirloom that belonged to an aunt—with nail scissors. Even at that age I could see that the wild color of the bedspread would make a super dress."

all the time I was growing up it did not occur to me that I could earn a living from something that was so much fun."

Despite Mary's early interest in fashion, her parents hoped she would become a teacher. Mary promised her parents she would earn an art teachers' license if they allowed her to study art. They agreed, and she attended Goldsmith's College in London. She never completed her teaching degree, but she did meet Alexander Plunket Greene, the man who would later become her husband and partner in a business that would shake the fashion world.

"Alexander and I . . . decided that we were not going to lead separate working lives," Mary Quant said of her relationship with Alexander Plunket Greene. "Somehow we would find a way of earning our living together."

THE CHELSEA MOVEMENT

After college, Quant moved out of her parents' house and took a job making hats for a Danish milliner. Life was a whirl of entertainment and friends. She and Greene were part of a growing movement of antiestablishment young people who were ready to change their own lives and the culture. Instead of following in their parents' footsteps by going to universities and becoming respectable businesspeople, they wanted to live free and unconventional lives. The area of London known as Chelsea developed into the center of this movement in Britain and gave it its name. There, in jazz clubs and coffeehouses, Greene and Quant socialized with young architects, painters, photographers, writers, and actors. They both cultivated an odd style of dress: Greene sometimes wore his mother's pajama tops as shirts, while Quant liked to mix unusual colors and patterns that were not typically worn together. She was spending most of her small salary on expensive dinners and parties, so she kept making her own clothes instead of buying them.

"People used to look at us wherever we went. They would laugh at us and sometimes shout after us, 'God, this Modern Youth!'"
—Mary Quant

BAZAAR, A BOUTIQUE

It was in Chelsea that Quant and Greene met Archie McNair, an ex-lawyer who loved the area and owned two successful businesses there—a photography shop and a coffee bar. Shortly after they met, Greene, McNair, and Quant thought that it would be fun to work together, so they decided to open a clothing boutique. McNair and Greene scraped together some money, and the trio rented the basement and first floor of a building called Markham House, located on King's Road in the center of Chelsea. Quant and Greene had no experience with business, but they were excited about the project. Quant began making hats and selling them while she and her partners planned their shop. She also visited nearby art schools, looking for talented young people who made just the right kinds of jewelry and accessories to sell in the boutique.

Quant's inexperience began to show. Clothing wholesalers she visited did not take her seriously because, with her wild style of dress, she looked more like a rebellious teenager than a business professional. Not knowing how to price the items they bought to sell in the boutique, Quant and her partners just tried to figure it out as best they could.

Despite these difficulties, the boutique, named Bazaar, opened in 1955. It was an instant sensation; merchandise seemed to fly off the shelves, and Quant and Greene had a hard time keeping the store stocked. It turned out they had priced their clothes so low that they were underselling all the nearby shops. Quant's wholesalers refused to sell her any more clothing because they were getting too many complaints from other stores. Bazaar soon had to raise its prices, but the clothes were still inexpensive—and as popular as ever.

LEARNING THE HARD WAY

Quant's only original designs in Bazaar's opening day inventory were a few hats and a pair of pajamas,

"I had always wanted the young to have fashions of their own . . . absolutely twentieth-century fashions . . . but I knew nothing about the fashion business."
—Mary Quant

but this quickly changed. She decided to design Bazaar's merchandise herself, though her business inexperience again became evident. Her manufacturing methods were as unconventional as her designs. She simply bought paper patterns and made them into new styles, then took classes on cutting. Not knowing that she could buy fabric wholesale for lower prices, Quant bought her materials at a department store, Harrods, and paid retail prices for them. She bought a sewing machine and hired a dressmaker to come to her apartment and sew the clothes. Each morning, she would take the money from the previous day's sales—the only money she had—to Harrods to purchase fabric. Her dressmaker then sewed the clothes during the day, and Quant took them to Bazaar at six that evening.

Word of mouth soon brought customers into the boutique in droves. Quant's saucy schoolgirl look— short, flared dresses worn with colored stockings and boots or flats—caught on quickly. Her designs were just what the customers wanted, and even the poorest working girls could afford them. Quant and Greene often kept Bazaar open until dawn, with friends and customers stopping by to shop after a night of dinner and dancing.

BOLD STOREFRONT WINDOWS

With business booming, Mary began to consider marketing strategies. She decided to put her store windows to work for her. She wanted to entertain people and get them talking about Bazaar, so she began creating window displays that would shock or

"We wanted everyone to like the shop and to like what we were doing. We wanted to appeal to husbands and boy friends as well as to the [women]. . . . We wanted them to say when walking down the King's Road to some restaurant or other, 'Let's walk past Bazaar and see what's happening!' We wanted the old ladies who had no intention of buying anything to stop and stare into the window and have some fun gossiping with their cronies about what a funny shop we were."
—Mary Quant

surprise passersby. Instead of using traditional mannequins, Quant had her mannequins made by a sculptor friend. She posed them in gawky, twisted positions similar to the trend in fashion photography at the time. One holiday window displayed stacks of milk bottles and a sign reading "Gone Fishing," with a mannequin dressed in holiday clothes vanishing through the back of the display. Another window held a mannequin with a real lobster on a leash. Although the entire store smelled of lobster, the

A woman watches Bazaar workers arrange a window display. Some passersby admired the displays, but others ridiculed them. Quant noticed, however, that "the more derisive the laughter at a new window display, the more things we were going to sell that week."

window did what it was designed to do—it forced passersby to notice Bazaar. Customers even began calling the store with window display ideas.

SUCCESS AND KNIGHTSBRIDGE

Around the time that Quant and Greene married in 1957, it was clear that Bazaar had become more than just a fun business to run. Chelsea was now well known as a fashion center and a hot spot for artists. Quant described it as "Britain's San Francisco, Greenwich Village, and the Left Bank. . . . A way of living and a way of dressing far more than a geographical area." The image of the "Chelsea girl" wearing knee-high leather boots, bright tights, and a short skirt was now recognized worldwide, and Bazaar provided the Chelsea girl's clothes. Young, working-class women loved Bazaar's inexpensive fashions, but the wealthy also flocked there for Mary Quant's designs, and even grown women started dressing like teenagers. The inclusion of her wild display in a large, formal fashion show in St. Moritz introduced Quant into the world of haute couture, further increasing the demand for her clothes.

Bazaar's success prompted Quant to open another boutique. She and Greene chose the Knightsbridge area of London as the location for the new shop. Knightsbridge was more expensive than Chelsea, but they were able to find a building with reasonable rent. When the Knightsbridge Bazaar opened, they had a huge press party, complete with a fashion show much like the one they had presented in St. Moritz. They displayed 40 outfits in 14 minutes, using a

"Once only the rich, the Establishment, set the fashion. Now it is the inexpensive little dress seen on the girls in the High Street."
—Mary Quant

"It was putting Bazaar right up amongst the top bracket at a time when my clothes were still considered pretty crazy outside Chelsea. The things I was making had nothing to do with accepted couture."
—Mary Quant, of the St. Moritz fashion show

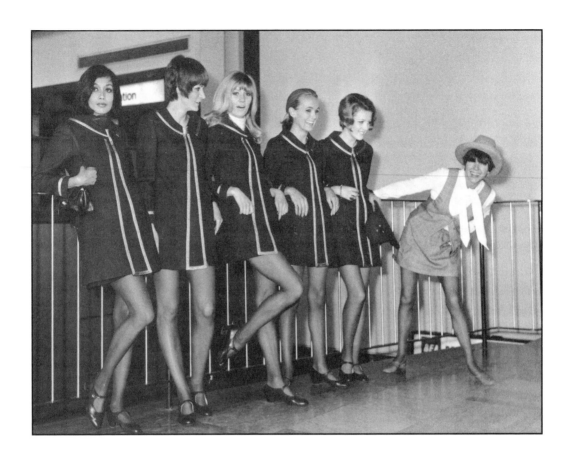

To display her designs, Quant tried to choose models who understood her style. She preferred photographic models, believing they moved more naturally and posed more dramatically than runway models. Quant is shown here with five of her models at London's Heathrow Airport, about to embark on a European fashion tour.

wind machine to swirl the models' skirts and create an even greater feeling of speed. The models carried outrageous props such as shotguns, dead pheasants, and oversized champagne glasses.

THE AMERICAN MARKET

Soon after that, Quant and Greene did what almost every top European designer eventually does—they took their products to the United States. In typical Quant fashion, they packed some garments in a suitcase and left for New York with a few telephone numbers. Their first meeting in New York ended disastrously when the fashion editor they were seeing called their clothes "crap." Sad but not defeated, they showed the collection to editors at *Women's Wear Daily*, one of the most important American fashion publications, and it printed a huge feature story about them. Excitement about their clothes spread through New York. Soon, it seemed everyone—including *Life* and *Seventeen* magazines—wanted to write an article about Mary Quant and her clothes.

Like Christian Dior before her, Quant returned home electrified from her American trip. Impressed by the high energy of New York City and the accurate sizing of the American manufacturers, she was eager to enter the American mass market. When the J. C. Penney company approached her about designing four collections a year for its department stores, she accepted the offer. For the first time, a British designer would be promoted through an American department store.

Penney's first order was for more than 6,000 garments, far too many for Quant's previous method of making her clothes. Leon Rapkin, a clothing manufacturer who ran a company called Steinberg's, helped Quant learn manufacturing techniques and adapt her designs for mass marketing. In 1963, Quant and Greene formed the Ginger Group Manufacturing Company to take care of assembling the clothes.

Experimental Designs

Quant's designs had become a force in the fashion world, and she began experimenting with new styles and fabrics. For a Paris fashion show, she designed what she called "The Wet Collection," using a material called polyvinyl chloride (PVC). PVC had never been used to make clothing before, and it caused a few manufacturing problems. The seams were welded at first, until Quant found that when the material cooled, they perforated and ripped apart like postage stamps. It took almost two years to devise a method of sewing the seams so that they stayed together. The shiny, brightly colored PVC clothes were widely popular—but by the time Quant perfected her manufacturing methods, other designers had begun to copy them. Quant later called the Wet Collection "the least commercially successful collection I ever made."

Quant was more successful in popularizing the miniskirt. After years of below-the-knee or knee-length dresses, miniskirts, at eight or nine inches above the knee, were truly a new style. Quant made them in flannels and fabrics with large bright designs, often using a daisy motif, which became her trademark. Sometimes she even adapted men's shirts and sold them as dresses. After raising the hems on skirts, she did the same for shorts. She invented very short shorts called hot pants, which were often worn with boots and patterned stockings.

Quant's daring designs and simple daisy logo linked her name with youth and freshness. They

polyvinyl chloride (PVC): a plastic-like substance used in various consumer goods such as raincoats and floor tiles

More than one designer claimed to have created the miniskirt. That argument might never be settled, but the miniskirt shown by the designer André Courrèges in 1964 was declared by *Vogue* magazine to be the shortest in Paris. "Maybe Courrèges did do miniskirts first, but if he did no one wore them," responded Mary Quant.

At left, model Jackie Bowyer displays a Mary Quant PVC raincoat and matching hat. At right, Mary Quant hot pants are modeled by Ann Goddett.

Beatle John Lennon (shown here with his wife, Cynthia Powell) launched a trend when he appeared in this Mary Quant hat in 1964. By the late 1960s, Quant's designs were also being worn by the model Twiggy, the actor Brigitte Bardot, and the singer Nancy Sinatra. Quant clothes also appeared in films such as Two for the Road (1967), starring Audrey Hepburn.

also fit right in with the experimental spirit of the 1960s. Young people were listening to new rock 'n' roll bands, such as the Beatles; creating "op art" and "pop art" in bold, colorful abstract forms; and wearing increasingly showy fashions. Vidal Sassoon's new bobbed hairstyles perfectly accented Quant's angular minidresses, and her midriff-baring cutout styles and wild stockings added drama to the Twist and the Jerk, popular dances of the period. Although the style Quant helped to create was first adopted by a group of fashion- and music-obsessed British youth known as "mods" (short for "modern"), the mod look soon caught on around the world. It was estimated that, by 1969, seven million women had a Quant label in their wardrobes.

Quant continued to experiment by expanding her business beyond clothing design. She created lines of affordable undergarments, hosiery, footwear, and cosmetics. As fashions began to change, she moved into housewares and linens, but it was her cosmetics line that would eventually become the most profitable and lasting part of her company. In the 1980s, Quant introduced unusual combinations such as blue nail polish and silver eyeliner. In 1994, when she turned 60, she opened a makeup boutique in London called the Mary Quant Colour Shop.

LEGACY

At the end of the year 2000, Mary Quant resigned from her position as the director of her company, Mary Quant Ltd. She sold her shares in the business—as well as the rights to the Mary Quant name

and daisy motif—to the Japanese businessmen who owned its cosmetics licensing agreements.

Mary Quant once said that her designs charted new areas. Women wearing Dior full skirts in 1950 never could have imagined that 10 years later skirts would barely cover their rear ends. Yet Quant not only visualized a new look of her own, but she also kept it fresh for a decade. Although her look died out in Britain and the United States, Quant's popularity remained strong among teenagers in Tokyo, Japan, who, at the dawn of the twenty-first century, wore short skirts, boots, and tights—much like the Chelsea girls of the 1960s.

Mary Quant poses with a wide range of her products—including shoes, makeup, and eyewear—in 1973.

In 2001, there were more than 200 Mary Quant Colour Shops in Japan, generating about $150 million in sales per year.

6

RALPH LAUREN

POLO FASHIONS

Ralph Lauren walked into Bloomingdale's department store in New York City and headed straight for the men's department. There was no time to linger over the store's suits and shirts; it was Father's Day 1968, his big debut. He stopped in front of a case filled with something new in the world of men's ties. These ties were fashioned from exquisite fabrics—English twills and Indian silks—in rich and satisfying colors, but it was the width of the ties that was unusual. Instead of the usual two inches, these ties were at least four inches wide! In a few minutes, Bloomingdale's customers would have their first chance to purchase the radical new Polo ties. Lauren had worked hard for this moment; Bloomingdale's had been reluctant to sell the ties with his name on

Combining a flair for fashion with a taste for tradition, Ralph Lauren (b. 1939) was the first to demonstrate that designing men's wear could be a creative and lucrative business.

them. But there they were, labeled "designed by Ralph Lauren" for all to see.

FROM LIFSHITZ TO LAUREN

On October 14, 1939, in a modest neighborhood in the Bronx, New York, Frieda Lifshitz gave birth to her fourth child, Ralph. Frieda and her husband, Frank, both Russian immigrants, raised Ralph and his brothers and sister in a conservative home, with an emphasis on a Jewish education. Frank Lifshitz painted houses for a living but drew his real satisfaction from painting murals. Frank was determined to be an American success. He decided Lauren would sound better than Lifshitz as the name of a great artist, so he changed the family's surname to Lauren.

Ralph inherited his father's drive for success, though as a boy he did not know it would lead him into the fashion world. Instead, he wanted to be a basketball player. "I didn't know what a fashion designer was in high school. . . . It was the last thing on my mind," he later said. The youngest of four children, Ralph often had to wear hand-me-downs, but he didn't mind. "Some of those clothes I really wanted, some of them I couldn't wait to get," he said.

As a teenager, Ralph Lauren was a snappy dresser. In his neighborhood, most kids dressed like their idols—such as movie star James Dean, who wore tight jeans, T-shirts, and leather jackets. But Lauren was not drawn to those fashions. He fantasized about how the wealthy classes lived, and he wore clothes that had an Ivy League or British feel to them, such as oxford shirts, crewneck sweaters, tweed trousers, or English sailor coats. Although these clothes were classic and traditional, Lauren also wanted them to have flair—a slightly wider collar, for instance, or a more fitted jacket. He carefully assembled his outfits, and when he could not find what he wanted in the high-class men's stores he shopped at, such as Brooks Brothers and Paul Stuart, he designed the clothes himself and had them made.

After high school, Lauren attended the City College of New York at night, working during the day at Alexander's, a nearby department store. Studying business in school, Lauren was bored. He already had a job, so why should he go to school? After two years at City College, he dropped out and began working as a salesman at Brooks Brothers. In the short time he was there, Lauren observed that wealthy people tended to be willing to pay more for high-quality clothes.

Then Lauren was drafted into the U.S. Army Reserves for six months. Upon his release, he took a job in the shipping department of Meyers Make, Inc., a manufacturer of gloves for men and women. Bored with his shipping job, Lauren asked for a chance to sell gloves. He worked energetically at his new job, but the old-fashioned gloves he was selling just weren't very popular anymore. In 1964, Lauren met Boston tie maker Abe Rivetz, who was looking for a salesman to represent his line in New York. Rivetz loved Lauren's unique sense of style, and Lauren knew this was his chance to move beyond selling gloves.

"Ralph always had ideas of what he wanted executed. . . . [He] was always quizzical, always asking why something wasn't done this way, always fantasizing about what he perceived as the world according to Ralph Lauren." —Clifford Grodd, president of Paul Stuart when Ralph Lauren shopped there

Henry Sands Brooks founded Brooks Brothers, a high-class men's clothing store, in 1818 in Manhattan. Brooks Brothers's many famous customers over the years included Abraham Lincoln and writer F. Scott Fitzgerald. The store became known for tweed jackets and soft-shouldered suits hinting of associations with the British aristocracy. Brooks Brothers was also one of the first stores to carry ready-to-wear clothes.

Lauren threw himself into his new job with enthusi-asm, but he soon learned that the world of ties was a very traditional and conservative one, with colors, patterns, and widths varying little from season to season. Lauren stood out among the tie salesmen at A. Rivetz and Company because he was decades younger than all the others and didn't dress like a typical conservative Boston man. His coworkers thought his wide-collared shirts and flared suits were too high-spirited.

With a keen eye on European fashion trends, Lauren soon realized that wider ties were becoming fashionable. He longed to design his own wide ties, but when he approached his bosses, he met with resistance. In the 1960s, the idea of "designing" a tie was absurd. The only thing tie manufacturers did was choose the colors. Basic tie shapes were already established, widths changed in fractions of an inch, and fabric manufacturers decided what fabrics would be used each season—who needed a designer?

Finally, frustrated at his bosses' reluctance to try something new, Lauren decided to start a company and design his own ties. To make this move he needed money. He looked for someone who believed in the marketability of an elegant wide tie and would invest in him. He found Ned Brower, the president of a tie company called Beau Brummell. When Brower heard about Lauren's plans, he decided to take the risk and back him financially. Brower had noticed the same industry changes that

Lauren had seen, and he knew Lauren's ties would not compete with his own conservative line. In 1967, Ralph Lauren became the president of Polo Fashions, his own division of Beau Brummell.

A LEVEL OF TASTE

Lauren recalled his time at Brooks Brothers to give him insight into the buying habits of wealthy people. "I'm promoting a level of taste, a total feeling," he said. "It's important to show the customer how to wear these ties, the idea behind the look." He chose the name of his company, Polo Fashions, with his customer in mind—the image of a polo player evoked a sense of old wealth and classic style. Lauren's ties would not only be wider and more elegant than any other ties available in New York, but they would also be exclusive. He knew that "if you buy expensive products, you don't want to see them all over the place." Most ties sold for less than $5, but Lauren's ties retailed for between $7.50 and $15. Lauren thought that his customers would be willing to pay more for ties made from high-quality fabrics, and that the higher price would make the ties seem even more special.

Lauren's strategy worked. Paul Stuart, a store at which he used to shop, was one of the first to buy his ties. Eventually, Polo ties gathered a following. Men who wore them recognized each other as they went about their lives, as if they were members of an elite club. By the time Bloomingdale's finally bought Lauren's ties in 1968, he was charging $15 to $20 per tie. As the demand for the ties spread, they soon caught the eye of someone who would influence the direction of Lauren's life.

MEN'S WEAR

Norman Hilton was the owner of Hilton Company, a manufacturer of men's suits since the late 1880s. Hilton first saw a Polo tie on one of his own salesmen, and he thought it was the ugliest thing he had ever seen. But then he started seeing Polo ties everywhere. When he discovered that they were being sold at Bloomingdale's, Hilton became interested. "Whoever is making those ties should be making them for Norman Hilton," he said. By the time Lauren and Hilton finished negotiating, Hilton had loaned Polo Fashions $50,000 and entered into a 50/50 partnership with Lauren. Lauren would not only design ties, but also men's suits, which the Hilton Company would manufacture.

Lauren wasted no time in getting started. Polo Fashions was incorporated on October 18, 1968. Just four days later, Ralph Lauren joined such famous designers as Oleg Cassini and Bill Blass in presenting his designs at the Creative Menswear Design Awards, held at the Plaza Hotel in New York. Lauren displayed only one suit. The jacket had a one-button closure and very wide lapels, and there were small pleats in the pants. This suit set the tone for Polo Fashions: the company would give customers classic clothing with a subtle flair, made from high-quality fabrics.

Even though Polo Fashions had begun as a division of Beau Brummell, Ned Brower allowed Lauren to keep the Polo name for his new venture with Norman Hilton.

HIS OWN VISION

Being the newcomer in the men's wear industry did not shake Lauren's confidence. Lauren made his decisions regardless of what the rest of the fashion industry was doing. When Norman Hilton suggested he look for a showroom in the New York building where most of the other men's wear designers were located, Lauren balked. How could he claim to offer a unique product if his company was just one of hundreds of men's wear companies listed on the building's directory? Lauren wanted to express a whole mood and way of life with his showroom—he couldn't be lost in a crowd of designers. Instead, he rented space in a residential building on 55th Street.

Lauren knew how he wanted things done, but because he had no formal design training, he did not sketch his designs. He had to rely on his ability to translate his ideas to the manufacturers. He described what he wanted and then modified the resulting garment, sometimes over and over, until the final product was perfect. Because of his unusual method of designing, Lauren often had conflicts with manufacturers, who became irritated with him for making so many miniscule changes to the designs. He never got along with Norman Hilton's top designer, Michael Cifarelli. Cifarelli made conservative, traditional suits and didn't understand Lauren's desire to make suits that flared out at the hip and jackets with soft, sloping shoulders.

"One day Ralph was in our factory discussing a suit with Cifarelli. The suit was on a dummy. Ralph was making these points, and Cifarelli was making other points. It wasn't terribly heated, because I don't think Ralph ever gets too excited. Cifarelli took the jacket off the form, carefully. Then he began to jump up and down on it. . . . So you can see it was a little difficult."
—Norman Hilton, on the relationship between Ralph Lauren and Michael Cifarelli

Even though he was new and young, Ralph Lauren never changed his style to suit the established men's wear designers and manufacturers. He had a vision of how his clothes should look. In 1969, that vision came to life when Lauren presented his first full line of men's wear. Then, after only two years of designing men's wear, Ralph Lauren was honored with a Coty Award, a prestigious fashion award, for best men's wear designer. This was only the second year that the award was given to a men's wear designer. The previous year Bill Blass had won

Ralph Lauren posing with some of his fashions—including his famous wide ties—in 1970

the award, and Lauren was ecstatic about being in the same class as such a famous designer.

A TOTAL LOOK

Other designers made only one kind of clothing, such as suits or ties, but Lauren thought that Polo Fashions should be about more than that. He wanted to create a total look for his customers. Lauren designed shirts, pants, and suits, but he also created raincoats, belts, and luggage. Whether a man was going to work in the city, flying to Europe on business, or spending a month on vacation at his country home, he could take Polo Fashions with him anywhere.

To promote his clothes as a complete image of a specific way of life, Lauren wanted Bloomingdale's to show his entire collection in a single Ralph Lauren boutique within its men's wear department. He thought that customers shouldn't just see his products individually; they should experience the whole mood his clothes evoked. Men's wear had never been merchandised in such a way before, and Bloomingdale's resisted. The department store agreed at last in 1970, and the boutique was designed to have the feel of a comfortable gentleman's club, with wood-paneled walls and worn leather chairs. Ralph Lauren was the first men's designer to have his own boutique in a department store.

Lauren took the boutique concept even further by allowing independent retailers to open their own Polo stores. Jerry Magnin, a men's wear retailer with a store in Beverly Hills, California, approached

A publicist named Eleanor Lambert came up with the idea for the Coty Award to enhance the prestige of the Coty Cosmetics Company. Beginning in 1943, the award was to be presented annually to a top American women's wear designer. The award was later given to multiple winners, one for best designer and others for different reasons, such as creativity. In 1969, Bill Blass became the first men's wear designer to receive a Coty.

Ralph Lauren about operating a store adjacent to his shop on Rodeo Drive, a fashionable shopping strip. Lauren agreed. He chose all the people for the store, from the interior designer to the manager, and Magnin went along, trusting Lauren. The interior designer used honey-colored wood, mirrors, skylights, and antique Persian rugs to create the same sense of old wealth that Lauren's collections reflected. The store opened in September 1971. Opening night was an elegant affair at which guests were served champagne and hors d'oeuvres and received special gifts commemorating the occasion.

> "The image we wanted to create was one of casual sportswear, and casual old money. It was to have a contemporary look, and yet it was to have a sense of tradition."
> —Tom O'Toole, designer of the first Polo store

MARKETING POLO

If the Polo store in Beverly Hills was innovative, Lauren's New York flagship store was a masterstroke of marketing. Lauren spent over $30 million to refurbish an elegant building on Madison Avenue known as the Rhinelander Mansion. Again designed with casual luxury in mind, this store showcased Ralph Lauren's entire collection. By opening his own store, Lauren made his retailers nervous. They thought their sales of Ralph Lauren clothes would drop because they would have to compete with Ralph Lauren himself for their customers' loyalty. Lauren disagreed, predicting that their sales would increase. After the store opened for business in April 1986, Lauren was proven right. Many in the fashion industry complimented Lauren for his incredible marketing skills, and the Rhinelander Mansion became a prominent New York tourist attraction, as well as a fashionable boutique.

Staying with his concept of selling a lifestyle, Ralph Lauren marketed his clothes with advertisements that told stories. "When I started, people thought they had to stand there with a suit and say, 'Here's my suit.' That's how the industry worked. I said, 'No, the clothes have to be there, but it's the mood that's important. . . . It's the image and mood of these people, who they are, what they feel like, you like them, and then you like what they wear.'"

The five-story Rhinelander Mansion was built in 1899. When he remodeled it for his store, Lauren decorated many of the sales areas as though they were rooms in a private home, with the clothing stored in antique dressers and chests. The store sold $31 million worth of merchandise in its first year of operation.

121

Ralph Lauren looking over fall ads with his staff in 1986. Lauren never liked television commercials as much as magazine advertising because he thought TV was too quick and the viewer had to be hit hard. Polo's method was more subtle than that, he said.

In his advertisements, Lauren used images of wealthy people caught in the midst of various activities. He bought large blocks of space in magazines, so he could advertise all of his collections at once. Lauren would often appear in Polo's advertisements himself—usually in his jeans and cowboy boots, instead of the tailored suit that the fashion industry expected. By doing the unexpected, Lauren created a sense of mystery around himself, which made people more interested in him and his clothes.

Chaps

It wasn't long before Ralph Lauren faced a problem encountered by all successful designers at some point in their careers—knock-offs. Because Lauren's clothes were so expensive, there was a large market for less costly versions of them. Manufacturers copied his designs and sold them for a fraction of the price of the originals.

In March 1971, Lauren responded to the challenge by creating a less expensive, more casual line, offering customers his designs at a price they could afford. Lauren based the new line on Western clothing, a style he enjoyed and often wore. Thanks to Hollywood Western films (such as those starring John Wayne), the American cowboy had become a hugely popular image.

Naming the line "Chaps" after the suede or leather pants-covers cowboys wore to protect their legs from thickets of brush while riding, Lauren made the clothes from soft, wearable fabrics like denim, corduroy, and flannel. Lauren hoped that by entering a new market, he would create more customers for his Polo lines, as well, when his loyal Chaps customers moved out of their jeans and into suits.

WOMEN'S WEAR

Although he had previously been reluctant to design for women, Lauren began thinking about it in 1971. It was common for women's wear designers to begin designing men's wear, but a men's wear designer had never branched out into designing women's wear. Persuaded by the encouragement of others, Lauren started with shirts based on his designs for men, but tailored for women and made from high-quality cotton and wool blends. Instead of using his Polo Fashions label, Lauren labeled his women's clothes "Polo by Ralph Lauren," which he hoped would give the line a personal touch. At the last minute, he added a polo player logo to the cuffs of the shirts.

Women loved the distinction of wearing Polo, and the shirts were an instant hit.

Lauren adapted more of his classic men's clothing into fitted jackets, skirts, suits, and pleated pants for women. He showed his first complete women's wear collection in May 1972, and the press loved it. Just two years later, Lauren won a Coty Award for women's wear, an amazing feat for a newcomer in a business with so many established designers.

One of Ralph Lauren's women's wear designs, from his 1979 fall/winter collection. The outfit was intended to resemble the traditional men's tuxedo.

Ralph Lauren's wife, Ricky Lowbeer—who he married in 1964—was the inspiration for many of his women's clothing designs. Unfortunately, since Ricky was very petite, this meant that most customers had trouble fitting into Lauren's narrow, streamlined clothes. They had to buy their outfits at least one size larger than usual—but they still bought them.

LICENSING

Norman Hilton sold his share of Polo Fashions to Ralph Lauren in December 1972, making Lauren the sole owner of the company. But by early 1973, Lauren was shocked to learn how much financial trouble Polo was in. He had turned the financial side of the business over to his friend Michael Bernstein in 1971, but Bernstein had been unable to salvage the tangled mess. Now, after years of management and production problems, Polo was close to bankrupt—despite its popularity and high level of sales (nearly $8 million in 1972).

Mia Farrow and Robert Redford in a scene from The Great Gatsby *(1974). Since the film was set in the 1920s, a period Lauren was already using as inspiration for his designs, costume designer Theoni Aldredge asked him to provide the outfits for Redford and the other male stars. The movie brought Lauren media attention and won an Academy Award for Best Costumes.*

Lauren had to do something. Top executives were resigning, and his credit was being turned down. Even though Polo was getting fabulous reviews and he had even been chosen to make the men's costumes for the film version of F. Scott Fitzgerald's novel *The Great Gatsby*, Lauren was having trouble making his payroll. In order to get the company back on its feet, Ralph Lauren licensed out his women's collection. Lauren would simply design the clothes, while a separate company manufactured and shipped them to buyers. Polo would receive a percentage of the profits from the sales. Lauren

eventually licensed out his Chaps line as well, and these two moves allowed Polo to begin making a profit again.

As the 1970s drew to a close, Lauren had learned how much money he could make by licensing his ideas. He knew it would be easy to do this with a fragrance, and the name recognition he acquired would increase sales of his other products. In Europe, designers Coco Chanel and Christian Dior had already put their names on scents. Launched in March 1978, Lauren's two fragrances—Polo for men and Lauren for women—were priced slightly higher than their competition to retain an air of exclusivity. Lauren had carefully chosen the scents and their packaging, refusing to launch the fragrances until everything was perfect. The Polo bottle featured simply a gold polo player on green glass, while the innovative, fruity Lauren scent was sold in a red glass bottle identified by the label "Lauren by Ralph Lauren." The fragrances were wildly successful, and Lauren eventually added a Chaps men's fragrance, which was sold to chain drugstores.

LEGACY

Ralph Lauren always stayed true to the image he first created for Polo Fashions, even as he branched into new markets. He introduced a sportswear collection and a home collection, which even included Ralph Lauren house paint. Lauren extended his business into European markets, as well. Polo opened a store in London in 1981, and his clothes became particularly popular in Japan. A children's clothing and accessories store opened in 1999 in London. Predictably, the store had an air of exclusivity, but Lauren carefully selected items that he thought would appeal to children—"combining classic looks with a strong sense of adventure," as he put it.

Ralph Lauren's high-school graduation yearbook was filled with teenage dreams. Some graduates yearned to become physicians, others scientists.

Models show off fashions from Ralph Lauren's spring 2001 men's wear collection.

Lauren's goal was summed up in one word—"millionaire." In 1993, 25 years after opening Polo Fashions, Ralph Lauren was estimated to be worth $700 million. By 2001, the Polo Ralph Lauren Corporation generated $4.8 billion in sales a year and operated 234 stores internationally, with another 108 run by licensees in more than 60 countries.

In addition to achieving his dream of wealth—hundreds of times over—Lauren also changed how fashion designers create and market their clothes. Department stores now house personal boutiques for many fashion designers, and designers commonly buy blocks of space in magazines for their advertisements. Men's wear designers are no longer wary of designing women's wear. And Ralph Lauren's clothing styles are imitated by American and European designers alike. All the while, Ralph Lauren continues to stand for classic, high-quality products for discerning customers.

"The thing that set Ralph apart was his single-mindedness of purpose. Everybody else moved from place to place, trend to trend. He wasn't trendy. What he did might have been trendy, but he stayed with it. It's the single most important thing about him. To this day there are people walking around saying Ralph Lauren isn't that special, I could have done it. It's the weirdest thing. They couldn't be more wrong. Ralph is the most special guy in the apparel business. He had integrity."
—Franklin Bober, a manager at Polo in 1974

7

VERA WANG

REVOLUTIONIZING BRIDAL WEAR

Dressed in her bridal finery, Vera Wang stepped back to look at her image in the mirror. Her jet-black hair, pulled into a simple clasp, flowed down her back. Her wedding dress, which weighed an amazing 25 pounds, was made of duchesse satin covered with tiny white beads and had fitted sleeves with buttons all down their lengths. An enormous fabric flower topped each sleeve. She should have been satisfied—after all, the dress had been custom-made at a cost of $10,000—but it still wasn't quite right. In 1989, however, all bridal dresses had the same elaborate style, and Wang didn't know what else she could do. "It was all even I knew about bridal at the time," she later said. By 1990, Vera Wang would have learned something about bridal

Popular among Hollywood stars, Olympic athletes, and other celebrities, the simple, elegant bridal gowns and eveningwear designed by Vera Wang (b. 1949) became the fashion sensation of the late 1990s and brought her small company international recognition.

wear. That year, she launched her signature line of bridal gowns, which would go on to become a huge success and make Vera Wang the most influential bridal designer in the United States.

DREAMING OF THE OLYMPICS

Vera Wang was born on June 27, 1949, in New York City. She probably would have been successful at just about anything she chose to do with her life, for she continually drove herself to do things well. Her parents set the example for their two children, Vera and her younger brother, Kenneth. Cheng Ching Wang, the children's father, arrived in the United States from China in the 1940s. For Cheng Ching, the U.S. represented the land of opportunity, and he set out to make the most of it. He built a hugely successful oil and pharmaceuticals company and settled his family in Manhattan. He and his wife, Florence Wu Wang, an interpreter for the United Nations, made sure their children knew they could be or do anything they wanted. They instilled in Vera and Kenneth a great respect for hard work and education, as well as a commitment to family. Vera took these lessons to heart.

Vera was only seven years old when she received a Christmas gift that would change her life—her first pair of ice skates. She quickly developed a love for skating that grew into dreams of competing as a world-class figure skater. Vera made up her mind to master the sport. She began getting up at six o'clock every morning to practice her skating before school. Determined to be the best, Vera worked steadily toward the ultimate figure-skating goal—competing in the Olympics.

As much as she loved figure skating, Vera believed that education was important. In 1968, she enrolled in Sarah Lawrence College as a pre-medical student. That same year, her hard work in skating began to pay off—she was allowed to compete in the U.S. National Figure Skating Championships. This was an exhilarating experience, giving Vera a taste of real competition. But her performance at the National Championships was not what she hoped. She soon realized that she could not train to compete in the Olympics and carry a full course of studies at the same time. She decided to give up competitive figure skating in order to finish her college education. Her disappointment proved overwhelming, however, and she suffered a complete breakdown in her sophomore year and had to leave school.

FASHION CALLS

Without skating or school, Vera Wang knew she needed to reevaluate her goals. She traveled to Paris to attend the Sorbonne (the University of Paris), where she studied art history and languages. This break turned out to be exactly what she needed. After a year in Paris, she returned to Sarah Lawrence to complete her degree in art history.

Visiting the Paris couture houses started Wang thinking about fashion. Wang had always loved shopping with her mother, who bought her clothes at famous couture houses, such as Chanel and Yves Saint Laurent. Wang's experience in choosing outfits for skating competitions had piqued her interest in clothing design. Realizing that fashion would "incorporate a lot of the things I loved," she became convinced that her future was in the apparel industry.

After several summers working as a salesperson and window dresser at the Yves Saint Laurent store in New York, Wang applied for a job at *Vogue* magazine. She arrived for her first assignment in what she thought was the height of fashion—a crepe Yves Saint Laurent dress and platform shoes—only to discover that she would be moving clothing racks and unpacking boxes for photo shoots. Although her first tasks were not very glamorous, Wang was promoted to fashion editor within two years and then to senior fashion editor. In these positions, she wrote about and analyzed fashion trends. After about 16 years with *Vogue*, she left for a position as design director at Ralph Lauren. Here, Wang immersed herself even more deeply in the fashion world, using her creative skills to enhance Lauren's designs.

With her professional life moving in a promising direction, Wang turned her attention to her personal life. Six months after their marriage in 1989, Wang and her husband, Arthur Becker, began trying to have a child. When Wang had trouble conceiving, she decided to start a harsh regimen of fertility treatments, which made it difficult for her to work. Her long hours and the strain of trying to start a family began to wear on her. Wang again decided to give up something she loved—she left Ralph Lauren after less than two years with the company.

Vera had always been close to her parents, and her father could tell how disappointed she was about giving up the Ralph Lauren job. He suggested she open her own business—a bridal boutique. This would allow her to be creative, yet control her own hours. She would be able to spend time being a wife and, hopefully, a mother.

Vera loved the idea of opening a bridal boutique, especially after her frustrating experience searching for a wedding gown. She knew she could help other brides who might also be having a hard time finding the right dress. "There was one basic look at the time: froufrou," she said. She planned to sell gowns that would make brides look and feel stylish and sophisticated, instead of like a doll on a wedding cake topper.

In 1990, Wang opened her boutique in the Carlyle Hotel in Manhattan. To put tense brides at ease, the store was designed to feel like a comfortable private home, decorated with overstuffed sofas, soft curtains, and fresh flowers. Wang emphasized personal, attentive customer service. Brides visited only by appointment, and they were assigned their own assistants who offered advice on caterers, invitations, and flowers in addition to helping select dresses. At first, Wang carried only gowns made by other designers. Gradually, however, Wang began designing gowns herself. She used luxurious silks and satins and intricate embroidery and beading. Her reputation spread from bride to bride.

Wang's dresses were a breath of fresh air to brides in the 1990s. She turned simple, classic designs—such as a frothy tulle skirt reminiscent of a ballet costume—into modern works of art with no fussy details. Instead, she used touches like a splash of rich color or a single floral embellishment. Her creations blended grace and dignity. "I design gowns with pure lines in luxe fabrics, but the simplest dresses are the most difficult to design [because] every seam shows," Wang said.

Vera Wang applauds her models after a showing of her 2001 wedding fashions.

The Wedding Gown

Even though at different times during history brides have worn white, a white wedding gown made to be worn only once was not common practice until the early twentieth century. In ancient Egypt, brides wore layers of pleated white linen, while ancient Greek brides, for whom white symbolized joy, wore white tunics. Roman brides wore saffron-colored (orange-yellow) veils to represent the flame of Vesta, the goddess of the home. Wealthy European brides in the fourteenth century wore richly colored gowns made from silk brocade or other precious fabrics. Brides who were less well-off rented their gowns.

The common practice for most European and American brides in the mid-nineteenth century was to wear brown or blue gowns that looked just like contemporary fashions. This way it was easy to wear the dresses again, with just a little adjustment. *Ladies' Home Journal* even recommended that brides use extra fabric in their wedding gowns so that they would "always be able to make it over into another style."

In 1840, Queen Victoria of England married her cousin Albert in a white gown of satin and lace. Although her gown was considered simple for a queen, it was made of costly materials and was very valuable, and the fashion magazines held it up as a standard for brides. This would start the trend toward white wedding gowns.

In the 1920s, Coco Chanel introduced a short white wedding gown in one of her collections. The dress featured a court train, a separate piece of fabric that attached to the shoulders of the dress. From that point on, brides wanted only one color for their wedding dresses: white.

Throughout the latter half of the twentieth century, wedding gowns went through many different styles, changing in accord with women's fashions. In the 1950s, women wore ankle-length wedding gowns made of nylon or organdy. When clothing became wildly colored and patterned in the 1960s, many brides wore cotton caftans and peasant smocks. But even in the 1960s, when miniskirts were at the height of their popularity, 87 percent of American women wore floor-length wedding gowns. In the 1980s, big white weddings, modeled after the wedding of Britain's beloved Princess Diana, became popular.

Despite the changes in wedding gowns throughout history, several common themes have endured. The white, floor-length wedding gown has continued to be popular into the twenty-first century. Modern wedding gown styles more often than not harken back to the Victorian period, with tightly fitted bodices and large, ballgown-like skirts. Queen Victoria's influence continues, both in style and in color.

Wang designed wedding gowns in every style, from suits to minidresses. One of her earliest gowns illustrated her innovative approach: a wide black velvet band edged the hem, neckline, and veil of an otherwise simple white dress, and matching velvet bows adorned the sleeves. Another dress featured a gold lace bodice, tulle sleeves, and a tulle ballerina-style skirt. Among her innovations was the use of "illusion" netting, which gave her dresses sensuality by making it look as if the bride was bare-skinned even though her skin was covered. Chet Hazzard—president of Wang's company, Vera Wang Bridal House Ltd.—said of her designs, "She balanced fashion edginess with traditional elegance."

BEYOND BRIDAL WEAR

Though Wang's initial success came from her work in bridal wear, she had always planned to use this as a steppingstone into broader markets. Wang made an easy transition into eveningwear. Her evening gowns immediately stood out, but without an in-your-face look. Celebrities began to notice her work and asked Wang to design their evening gowns for special occasions. Her big break came when Best Actress nominee Sharon Stone wore an old-fashioned satin Wang ballgown to the 1993 Academy Awards ceremony. Fashion designers receive an enormous amount of publicity on "Oscar night," as the ceremony is called. Movie stars spend months planning their entire Oscar night look, and the media pays almost as much attention to which designers' clothes are worn as to who wins an Oscar.

Stone's gown was much admired, securing Wang's reputation as an A-list Hollywood designer. She went on to dress many of the world's most fashionable women—such as Holly Hunter, Meg Ryan, Uma Thurman, Helen Hunt, Mariah Carey, and Tyra Banks—for the Oscars and other events. Her most well-known successes included a form-fitting, strapless satin gown with matching cape worn by Jane Fonda, and a simple blue column dress with a front slit worn by Sarah Michelle Gellar.

Along with designing dresses, Vera Wang sometimes offered other fashion suggestions to her clients. She advised Jane Fonda to cut her hair in a new shag style to go with this strapless satin gown for the 2000 Oscars. The cut and the gown were a huge success, bringing Fonda renewed popularity.

All this success meant a grueling schedule, but Wang still found time to relax with her husband and their two daughters, Cecilia and Josephine (adopted after the couple ceased fertility treatments in 1991). Skating, still important to Wang years after she gave up her Olympic figure-skating dreams, found its way into her life in a different, unexpected way: she designed costumes for champion figure skater Nancy Kerrigan for the 1992 and 1994 Olympic Games. While thousands watched Kerrigan's performances, they could not help but notice her costumes. In contrast to most skating outfits, which were flashy

Vera Wang poses in a swimming pool with her husband, Arthur Becker, and their children, Cecilia (left) and Josephine.

and spangled, Wang's designs for Kerrigan were subtle, elegant, and modern. Wang's influence revolutionized skating costumes as other skaters rushed to imitate Kerrigan's look. The Olympics brought Wang tremendous exposure and increased name recognition, prompting other major designers—such as Christian Lacroix and Donna Karan—to follow her lead in creating skating fashions. Wang continued to design costumes, including Michelle Kwan's outfits for the 2002 Olympics.

Nancy Kerrigan performs in one of her Vera Wang outfits during the 1994 Winter Olympics. "It's all the worst things combined together technically," Wang said of designing figure-skating costumes. "The skater has to look like she's in an evening gown . . . [but] she's got to be able to do triple jumps and not rip."

Wang continued to expand into other markets, including ready-to-wear, fur, and footwear. She also developed a signature fragrance. These products and her dresses (which ranged in price from $2,000 to $20,000) sold in a number of high-end department stores around the United States. But Wang didn't leave the bridal industry behind. She opened a second New York boutique, this time showcasing

Wang's fall 2000 ready-to-wear collection included this ensemble of a leather coat, cashmere silk top, and skirt.

A model shows a dress from Wang's fall 2001 bridal collection. The gown is made of three layers of chiffon georgette and tulle, each individually draped, beaded in an abstract floral pattern.

her bridesmaid collections, and published her own wedding guidebook, *Vera Wang on Weddings*.

Wang's effort to change bridal gowns from frothy confections into elegant works of art for modern women resulted in a revolution in bridal wear. Her simple but elegant designs allowed brides to choose a sophisticated, tasteful dress for their wedding day. Wang's evening creations, while bearing her stamp of simple elegance, also allowed the wearer's own personality to shine.

"I think that in my clothes, people see you, they don't only see the dress. I believe that if your clothes wear *you*, it isn't modern. I'm after much more subtlety. I want the woman and her personality, her own eccentricity and her own sense of self to come through."
—Vera Wang

143

OTHER BUSINESS BUILDERS IN FASHION

Cristóbal Balenciaga (1895-1972) began as a tailor in Spain before moving to Paris in 1937 to direct his own couture house. His clothes—chemises, tunics, suits with boxy bolero-like jackets, narrow skirts, coats, and capes—were simple and skillfully made, flattering the body while retaining their own geometric forms. Often called "fashion's Picasso," Balenciaga was considered the main rival of Christian Dior. He closed his business and retired in 1968; new owners revived the House of Balenciaga in the 1980s.

Anne Klein (1921-1974) launched Junior Sophisticates in 1948, transforming the American junior-sized clothing market by giving young women a more adult look. In 1968, she opened Anne Klein & Co., which produced elegant but practical sportswear for working women. Klein pioneered separates dressing, in which simple, interchangeable articles of clothing—including blazers, shirtdresses, and trousers—were coordinated together and complemented with accessories to create a finished, no-fuss look. She also began the practice of selling her designs in boutiques within major department stores.

Pierre Cardin (b. 1922) helped design Dior's "New Look" before opening his own couture house in Paris in 1950. He is known for designing minimalist, sculptural clothes that had their own structure and stood away from the body. He shocked the couture world by opening a ready-to-wear line in 1959 and then moving into men's wear—where his high-buttoned collarless jackets, worn by the Beatles in the 1960s, showed that men's suits could be high fashion. A shrewd entrepreneur, Cardin was the first designer to open markets in Japan, China, Russia, and Romania. With more than 600 licenses for products from ties to frying pans, Cardin may be the world's richest fashion designer.

Hubert de Givenchy (b. 1927) opened his own Paris house in 1952, designing simple, refined clothes with strong lines (much like his idol and friend, Balenciaga). He also adopted the concept of separates introduced by American designers such as Anne Klein. Givenchy is best known for providing actor Audrey Hepburn's chic day and evening gowns, tailored suits, sophisticated coats, cocktail dresses, and whimsical hats for films such as *Sabrina* (1954) and *Breakfast at Tiffany's* (1961), as well as her personal wardrobe.

Liz Claiborne (b. 1929) started her own company in 1976 to make clothing for American working women. Her innovative sportswear and dress designs were so successful that the company began publicly selling stock in 1981 and eventually expanded into shoes, accessories, jeans, men's wear, fragrances, plus-size clothing, activewear, and eyewear. With 26 brands and more than 400 specialty and outlet stores, Liz Claiborne, Inc., is the fourth-largest apparel company in the world.

Giorgio Armani (b. 1934) introduced his first men's wear collection in Italy in 1974, seeking to restructure the traditional tailored suit jacket by eliminating linings and shoulder pads. The result was simple, flexible clothing—navy blazers, linen jackets, oversized overcoats and raincoats—that looked relaxed but was still made with luxurious, high-quality fabric. Armani launched a similar line of women's wear in 1975, and in the 1980s he expanded into less expensive sportswear lines. His company has about 260 stores in more than 30 countries and is the best-selling brand of European design in the United States.

Yves Saint Laurent (b. 1936) took over the House of Dior in 1957, when he was just 21 years old. After rocketing to fame with his innovative "trapeze" dress, which had underskirts that made it appear to float away from the body, he opened his own Paris couture house in 1962. In 1966, he launched the first in a chain of 172 Rive Gauche boutiques selling ready-to-wear clothes—a move that brought French fashion to a wider audience and was later imitated by other designers. Saint Laurent retired in 2002.

Calvin Klein (b. 1942), perhaps the most successful and well-known American designer, founded his own company in 1968 and soon became identified with understated, comfortable, and streamlined clothes. Klein is famous for his designer jeans, underwear, and fragrances (including the first fragrance for both men and women, CKOne), as well as for the controversial TV and print advertisements he used to promote them. His products generate more than $5 billion per year in retail sales.

Donna Karan (b. 1948) dedicated herself to meeting women's fashion needs for everyday work and play. After heading Anne Klein & Co. following its founder's death in 1974, she founded Donna Karan New York in 1985 and then launched the less expensive DKNY label for younger women. Her trademarks include bodysuits, wrap-around skirts, and the use of materials such as black cashmere and stretch fabrics—all designed to be comfortable, durable, artistic, and flattering for women of all body types. Her company, Donna Karan International (which also sells men's wear, accessories, and shoes), was purchased by fashion conglomerate LVMH in November 2001.

Tommy Hilfiger (b. 1952) established his line of colorful, classic, clean-cut men's sportswear in the 1980s. By the 1990s, the popularity of Hilfiger's designs—particularly among urban youth—had made him one of the leading names in American fashion. His company publicly offered shares of stock in 1992, introduced a line of tailored clothing in 1994, and later expanded into women's wear, children's wear, and accessories.

GLOSSARY

bodice: the upper part of a woman's dress, which extends from her waist to her shoulders and is usually fitted

bolero: a short jacket worn open in front

boutique: a small business offering specialized products or services, particularly a small retail store selling fashionable clothing

breeches: men's pants that end at the knee, often worn for horseback riding

brocade: a heavy fabric with a detailed, raised design

bustle: a wire and fabric accessory worn at the back of a skirt to create fullness

cabaret: a nightclub that provides short programs of live entertainment

cardigan: a type of knitted sweater that opens down the front, usually with buttons as closures

chaps: suede or leather pants-covers worn by cowboys to protect their legs from thickets of brush while riding

corset: an undergarment that fits around a woman's torso and usually contains strips of bone or metal (called stays) for stiffening, worn to tighten and shape the waist and hips

costume jewelry: jewelry made from imitation stones rather than precious gems

couturier: a designer who creates haute couture; *see also* **haute couture**

crinoline: a steel or whalebone cage worn under a woman's skirt to give it fullness

draper: a dealer in cloth

dry goods: textiles, clothing, and other related items

Fair Isle sweater: a specific type of sweater from Scotland, usually made of wool and characterized by colorful geometric patterns

finishing school: a private girls' school that teaches young women how to run a household and behave correctly at social functions

haute couture or **couture:** (from French, meaning "high or elegant sewing") fashion created exclusively for one person; also the designers and establishments that create this fashion

jersey: a soft, knitted fabric

license: to authorize the use of one's name or ideas, usually in exchange for a flat fee or royalties

loincloth: a strip of fabric worn over the loins, or pelvic area

manufacturer: one who owns or operates a large-scale factory or industrial operation that makes a raw material (in fashion, fabric) into a finished product (clothing)

mercer: a dealer in textiles, especially silks; *see also* **textile**

millinery: a hat shop

patent: government recognition that an invention belongs to a particular inventor, which gives the inventor the sole right to produce and sell the invention for the duration of the patent

pattern: a template, usually made of tissue paper, used as a guide when cutting and sewing material to make clothing

petticoat: starched underskirts worn beneath an outer skirt to create fullness

pleat: a fold made by doubling material onto itself and then sewing it in place

polyvinyl chloride (PVC): a plastic-like substance used in various consumer goods such as raincoats and floor tiles

ready-to-wear: clothing that is manufactured in standard sizes and then sold to customers off the rack in the store

retail: to sell goods in small amounts directly to consumers

sumptuary law: a law that assigns dress styles based on income, usually for the purpose of restricting lavish dress

tailor: one who makes and repairs clothing

textile: a fabric, especially one made by weaving or knitting

toga: a loose piece of fabric wrapped around the body in elaborate folds, worn by the Romans during the time of the Roman Empire

toile: a dress made of less expensive fabrics, such as linen or canvas, that serves to show a designer how well a design will work

tulle: a fine, netlike, often starched fabric used to make veils, tutus, and gowns

wholesale house: a place that sells goods to retailers, usually in large quantities, for resale in their stores

BIBLIOGRAPHY

Blum, Stella, ed. *Victorian Fashions and Costumes from Harper's Bazar, 1867-1898.* New York: Dover, 1974.

Buttolph, Angela. *The Fashion Book.* London: Phaidon, 1998.

Calasibetta, Charlotte. *Fairchild's Dictionary of Fashion.* New York: Fairchild, 1975.

Carnegy, Vicky. *Fashions of a Decade: The 1980s.* New York: Facts On File, 1990.

Connikie, Yvonne. *Fashions of a Decade: The 1960s.* New York: Facts on File, 1990.

Constantino, Maria. *Men's Fashion in the Twentieth Century: From Frock Coats to Intelligent Fibres.* New York: Costume and Fashion Press, 1997.

Contemporary Fashion. New York: St. James, 1995.

Cunnington, C. Willett. *English Women's Clothing in the Nineteenth Century.* New York: Dover, 1990.

Daves, Jessica. *Ready-Made Miracle: The American Story of Fashion for the Millions.* New York: Putnam, 1967.

de la Haye, Amy, and Shelley Tobin. *Chanel: The Couturiere at Work.* New York: Overlook, 1996.

de Marly, Diana. *Christian Dior.* New York: Holmes & Meier, 1990.

———. *The History of Haute Couture, 1850-1950.* New York: Holmes & Meier, 1980.

———. *Worth: The Father of Haute Couture.* New York: Holmes & Meier, 1990.

Dior, Christian. *Christian Dior and I.* Translated by Antonia Fraser. New York: Dutton, 1957.

Downey, Lynn. "Founder." http://www.levistrauss.com/about/bio.html, cited January 28, 2002.

———. "History of Denim." http://www.levistrauss.com/about/denim.html, cited January 28, 2002.

Earle, Alice Morse. *Two Centuries of Costume in America: MDCXX-MDCCCXX.* New York: Benjamin Blom, 1968.

Ewing, Elizabeth. *History of Twentieth Century Fashion.* Totowa, N.J.: Barnes and Noble, 1986.

Fallon, James. "Lauren's 1st Kids' Store Makes Debut in London." *Women's Wear Daily*, December 14, 1999.

Feldman, Elane. *Fashions of a Decade: The 1990s.* New York: Facts on File, 1992.

Galante, Pierre. *Mademoiselle Chanel.* Translated by Eileen Geist and Jessie Wood. Chicago: H. Regnery, 1973.

Gillian, Audrey. "Mary Quant Quits Fashion Empire." *The Guardian,* http://www.guardianunlimited.co.uk, cited December 12, 2001.

Gross, Michael. "Ralph's World." *New York,* September 20, 1993.

Hall, Lee. *Common Threads: A Parade of American Clothing.* Boston: Little, Brown, 1992.

Henry, Sondra, and Emily Taitz. *Everyone Wears His Name: A Biography of Levi Strauss.* Minneapolis: Dillon, 1990.

Hunt, Alan. *Governance of the Consuming Passions: A History of Sumptuary Laws.* New York: St. Martin's, 1996.

Jarnow, Jeanette, and Beatrice Judelle. *Inside the Fashion Business.* New York: John Wiley, 1965.

Laver, James. *Costume and Fashion: A Concise History.* London: Thames and Hudson, 1995.

"The Look of Vera Wang." *In Style,* December 2000.

Lynam, Ruth. *Couture: An Illustrated History of the Great Paris Designers and Their Creations.* Garden City, N.Y.: Doubleday, 1972.

McBride-Mellinger, Maria. *The Wedding Dress.* New York: Random House, 1993.

Madsen, Axel. *Chanel: A Woman of Her Own.* New York: Holt, 1990.

Martin, Richard, and Harold Koda. *Haute Couture.* New York: The Metropolitan Museum of Art, 1995.

Miller, Sue, and Cynthia Sanz. "Chic to Chic." *People,* July 20, 1998.

Olian, JoAnne. "Charles Frederick Worth: The Founder of Haute Couture." http://www.mcny.org/worth.htm, cited January 7, 2002.

Pochna, Marie-France. *Christian Dior: The Man Who Made the World Look New.* New York: Arcade, 1994.

Quant, Mary. *Quant by Quant.* London: Cassel, 1966.

Rubin, Leonard. *The World of Fashion: An Introduction.* New York: Harper, 1976.

Sample, Ann. "Designer to the Stars, Vera Wang." *Women to Watch.* http://www.womenswire.com/watch/wang.html, cited November 18, 2001.

Saunders, Edith. *The Age of Worth: Couturier to the Empress Eugenie.* Bloomington, Ind.: Indiana University Press, 1955.

Steele, Valerie. "Exhibition Review: Christian Dior. The Costume Institute. The Metropolitan Museum of Art." *Fashion Theory: The Journal of Dress, Body & Culture*, June 1997.

Trachtenberg, Jeffrey A. *Ralph Lauren: The Man Behind the Mystique.* Boston: Little, Brown, 1988.

"Vera Wang." *The Asian American Woman.* http://AsiaMs.net/Fashion/WangVera/vwang.html, cited July 16, 2002.

Wallach, Janet. *Chanel: Her Style and Her Life.* New York: Nan A. Talese, 1998.

Wood, Dana. "Unveiling Vera." *W*, September 1998.

Worth, Jean Philippe. *A Century of Fashion.* Boston: Little, Brown, 1928.

SOURCE NOTES

Quoted passages are noted by page and order of citation.

Chapter One

p. 21 (both): Diana de Marly, *Worth: The Father of Haute Couture* (New York: Holmes & Meier, 1990), 105.

p. 26 (margin): JoAnne Olian, "Charles Frederick Worth: The Founder of Haute Couture," http://www.mcny.org/worth.htm, cited January 7, 2002.

p. 37 (margin): Elizabeth Ewing, *History of Twentieth Century Fashion* (Totowa, N.J.: Barnes and Noble, 1986), 15.

Chapter Three

p. 61: Axel Madsen, *Chanel: A Woman of Her Own* (New York: Holt, 1990), 105.

p. 64 (margin): Madsen, *A Woman of Her Own*, 133.

p. 66 (caption): Pierre Galante, *Mademoiselle Chanel*, translated by Eileen Geist and Jessie Wood (Chicago: H. Regnery, 1973), 213.

p. 66 (first): Madsen, *A Woman of Her Own*, 163.

p. 66 (second): Madsen, *A Woman of Her Own*, 163.

p. 67 (both): Madsen, *A Woman of her Own*, 198.

p. 68: Amy de la Haye and Shelley Tobin, *Chanel: The Couturiere at Work* (New York: Overlook, 1996), 42.

p. 69 (margin): House of Chanel.

pp. 70-71: Galante, *Mademoiselle Chanel*, 200.

p. 71 (first): Marie-France Pochna, *Christian Dior: The Man Who Made the World Look New* (New York: Arcade, 1994), 144.

p. 71 (second, third, fourth): Madsen, *A Woman of Her Own*, 288.

p. 71 (fifth): Madsen, *A Woman of Her Own*, 323.

p. 72 (margin): Madsen, *A Woman of Her Own*, 124.

Chapter Four

p. 79 (margin): Pochna, *Man Who Made the World Look New*, 63.

p. 82 (first): Christian Dior, *Christian Dior and I*, translated by Antonia Fraser (New York: Dutton, 1957), 16.

p. 82 (second): Dior, *Christian Dior and I*, 39.

p. 86 (first): Valerie Steele, "Exhibition Review: Christian Dior. The Costume Institute. The Metropolitan Museum of Art," *Fashion Theory: The Journal of Dress, Body, & Culture*, June 1997, 233.

p. 86 (second): Pochna, *Man Who Made the World Look New*, 135.

p. 87 (margin): Diana de Marly, *Christian Dior* (New York: Holmes & Meier, 1990), 19.

pp. 88-89: Pochna, *Man Who Made the World Look New*, 180.

p. 91: Pochna, *Man Who Made the World Look New*, 245.

Chapter Five

p. 96 (margin): Mary Quant, *Quant by Quant* (London: Cassel, 1966), 17-18.

p. 96: Quant, *Quant by Quant*, 17.

p. 97 (caption): Quant, *Quant by Quant*, 16.

pp. 97-98: Quant, *Quant by Quant*, 16.

p. 98 (caption): Quant, *Quant by Quant*, 36.

p. 99 (margin): Quant, *Quant by Quant*, 31.

p. 100 (margin): Ruth Lynam, *Couture: An Illustrated History of the Great Paris Designers and Their Creations* (Garden City, N.Y.: Doubleday, 1972), 179.

p. 101 (margin): Quant, *Quant by Quant*, 47.

p. 102 (caption): Quant, *Quant by Quant*, 47.

p. 103 (first margin): Quant, *Quant by Quant*, 75.

p. 103 (second margin): Quant, *Quant by Quant*, 79.

p. 103: Quant, *Quant by Quant*, 73.

p. 105: Quant, *Quant by Quant*, 104.

p. 106 (margin): Lynam, *Couture*, 198.

p. 106: Quant, *Quant by Quant*, 126.

Chapter Six

p. 112 (both): Jeffrey A. Trachtenberg, *Ralph Lauren: The Man Behind the Mystique* (Boston: Little, Brown, 1988), 23.

p. 113 (margin): Trachtenberg, *Ralph Lauren*, 29.

p. 115 (first): Trachtenberg, *Ralph Lauren*, 45.

p. 115 (second): Trachtenberg, *Ralph Lauren*, 56.

p. 116: Trachtenberg, *Ralph Lauren*, 57.

p. 117 (margin): Trachtenberg, *Ralph Lauren*, 64.

p. 120 (margin): Trachtenberg, *Ralph Lauren*, 80.

p. 121: Trachtenberg, *Ralph Lauren*, 218.

p. 128: James Fallon, "Lauren's 1st Kids' Store Makes Debut in London," *Women's Wear Daily*, December 14, 1999, 16.

p. 129 (margin): Trachtenberg, *Ralph Lauren*, 154.

p. 129: Trachtenberg, *Ralph Lauren*, 27.

Chapter Seven

p. 131: Sue Miller and Cynthia Sanz, "Chic to Chic," *People*, July 20, 1998, 134.

p. 134 (both): Miller and Sanz, "Chic to Chic," 133.

p. 135: Miller and Sanz, "Chic to Chic," 134.

p. 136: Maria McBride-Mellinger, *The Wedding Dress* (New York: Random House, 1993), 100.

p. 137: McBride-Mellinger, *The Wedding Dress*, 30.

p. 138: McBride-Mellinger, *The Wedding Dress*, 100.

p. 141 (caption): "Vera Wang," *The Asian American Woman,* http://AsiaMs.net/Fashion/WangVera/vwang.html, cited July 16, 2002.

p. 143 (margin): Dana Wood, "Unveiling Vera," *W*, September 1998, 239.

INDEX

ABOUT THE AUTHOR

Jacqueline C. Kent is a Jamaican-born author, freelance writer, and homeschooling mom. She is the author of two other books from The Oliver Press, *Women in Medicine* and *Business Builders in Cosmetics*. She has a master's degree in Latin American history and gender studies and lives with her husband and two children in Reno, Nevada.

PHOTO CREDITS